A HISTORY
OF HENDON

A HISTORY
OF HENDON

John Hopkins

HENDON BOROUGH COUNCIL
1964

Designed and printed in Great Britain by
W. S. Cowell Ltd, at the Butter Market, Ipswich

CONTENTS

ACKNOWLEDGEMENTS

This history is based very largely on material in the Local History Collection and in the collection of the Mill Hill and Hendon Historical Society housed at Hendon Central Library. It forms therefore a tribute to the late Miss Elsie Pyman, who was Reference Librarian at Hendon, from 1 July 1929 to 25 August 1956 and who, during that time, devoted much dedicated care and attention to the acquisition of material concerned with Hendon's history. I have also received considerable assistance from members of the Mill Hill and Hendon Historical Society and the Hendon and District Archaeological Society and from Mr E. G. Barnes who kindly provided material on the early history of the railways in Hendon. The files of the *Hendon & Finchley Times* have proved an invaluable mine of information and I am grateful too for the help and encouragement I have received from the Borough Librarians under whom I have worked, J. E. Walker, K. C. Harrison and S. J. Butcher.

INTRODUCTION

This brief history of Hendon* is intended, not for the specialist, but for the ordinary man in the street who would like to know a little more about the history of the borough in which he lives. In compressing the story into so short a length it is obvious that much has been omitted. To assist those who would like to pursue their studies further I have added a select bibliography of printed works at the end of this volume. All of these are in the Local History Collection at the Hendon Central Library as are many of the manuscript sources which have been used.

I have attempted to tell in a connected and chronological sequence the outline of the history of Hendon and of the people who have lived here. An area which has been found by many thousands of ordinary citizens a pleasant place to live.

* The term Hendon in this work indicates the modern Borough of Hendon as it was constituted in the Charter of 1932.

The place name Hendon derives from two Anglo-Saxon words *Heah* and *dun* which in the form *Heandun* means *At the high down*.

THE BEGINNINGS TO
THE CONQUEST

Situation and description

The present Borough of Hendon lies in the north-west corner of Middlesex and is about seven miles long and nearly four miles wide at its widest point. Its northern end rests on the heights of the north-west Middlesex highlands and the southern end reaches up to the high ground of Hampstead. There are two ridges running down from the northern heights, one through Totteridge and the other running through Highwood Hill into Mill Hill village. Apart from these ridges, there is an isolated hill at Church End lying between the Silk and Brent streams which run together at the Welsh Harp. The lower ground between the two main heights is well watered by these streams and their tributaries.

Geology

The great basin between the Chiltern Hills and the North Downs is composed of chalk and is known as the London Basin. This deposit was built millions of years ago, when the whole of this area was many fathoms beneath the sea. Later this chalk was raised above the sea level and began to be worn away by the action of rain and flood, though not to any great extent, as, geologically speaking, this exposure was not for long and the chalk was once again covered by the sea. This time the depth was not so great and the chalk became covered by a layer of clay.

Later, when the depth of water was even shallower, a layer of gravel and sand was deposited on top of the clay. As the whole area was again lifted above the sea this top deposit of sand was washed away by the rivers in the valleys, and today only remains as pockets on high ground as at Church End and Highwood Hill.

Hendon before the coming of the Romans

We know very little for certain about Hendon before the Roman invasion, but you must imagine Middlesex as large stretches of forest with small villages here and there. These were on the higher ground, as the low-lying ground in the river valleys was extremely marshy. The rivers were wider than they are now, and in times of flood the ground near the river was covered by large sheets of water which only slowly drained away. Some patches of cultivation would have existed in woodland glades, for the land was fertile, if heavy, and these clearings would be slowly growing as the population increased.

The earliest people living in Middlesex of whom much is known were Neolithic men, and remains of their culture have been found in the county. These are tools and weapons of stone. When these people lived in Middlesex, England was still joined to the continent of Europe and where the North Sea is now was dry land. Our present coastline was not arrived at until some 8,000 years ago.

Between about 1300 B.C. and 150 B.C. three waves of Celtic invaders from western Europe displaced the earlier settlers. The third of these waves, who settled most of south-east England, was of tribes who came from the area between the Rhine and the Seine, and who were called Belgae. When these tribes arrived in Britain they tended to keep the name by which they had been previously known. The tribe that settled in Middlesex were known as the Catuvellauni.

The Catuvellauni were a warlike tribe. They dressed in woollen clothes, for they understood the arts of spinning and weaving, and the pattern of their cloth resembled a tartan. They wore breeches drawn tight at the ankles. They were great hunters and the forests were well stocked with deer, boars and wolves. Their houses were crude cabins of logs and reeds, and these were gathered in townships which were protected by a ditch and a rampart. They kept considerable herds of cattle which grazed in the forests, and which they drove into large enclosures at night or when danger threatened. They used both iron and bronze for weapons and tools. Bronze enamel ware was used for decoration and gold, silver and copper coins were current. Their agriculture was carried on in scattered patches, rather than in regular shaped fields, and they grew wheat, barley and millet. They kept sheep, goats and pigs, and bees were kept in wicker hives, for these early Britons were expert basket makers.

Trackways

Even before the Romans came, trade was being carried on between Britain and Gaul across the narrow Channel, and the merchants trod trackways in their search for trade. Then, as now, they would have landed near Dover and their track led along the high ground bordering the Thames, probably crossing at the first main ford, which is where the Brent joins the Thames at Brentford, although it is possible they also used a minor ford near Westminster. On the other side of the river at Brentford these trackways branched east, west and north, and the northern track, leading to what is now St Albans, probably ran along the western edge of Hendon, where the Romans later built their Watling Street, the road which we now know as the Edgware Road. Here and there along the road camps were built. In peaceful times these would serve as shelters for the traders, and in wartime as fortified encampments. There was such a stronghold on Brockley Hill, just beyond the borders of Hendon at Stanmore.

Trade

Merchants coming from Gaul traded in corn, cattle and hides, gold, silver, iron, slaves and dogs. These hounds from this part of Britain were famous for their strength and skill in hunting, and one breed were said to be strong enough to bring down an ox.

The coming of the Romans

The power of the Roman Empire had spread across Europe into Gaul, and in 55 B.C. Julius Caesar made his first attempt at an invasion of Britain. This first attempt was a failure, for Caesar arrived with far too small an army and he scarcely penetrated more than ten miles inland from Dover. In the following year, however, he came with a stronger force and drove his way inland, and, following the old trackway, forced a passage of the Thames at Brentford in the face of strong opposition. He defeated the Catuvellauni, who made a stand at Brockley Hill, and penetrated deep into their territory. The legions' ordered lines proved too much for the undisciplined mass of British infantry and chariots, skilfully as these were used. In his march north Caesar probably used the old trackway running to St Albans (following roughly the line of the present Edgware Road) and was harassed in his advance by the tribesmen, who used the cover of the forests for ambushes and raids.

The uprising of the tribes in Gaul diverted attention from Britain, and Caesar withdrew, after exacting tribute, to put this rebellion down. The continuing struggle for power in Rome, and the ensuing civil wars, prevented any further Roman invasions for another hundred years. However, Roman influence was still strong, for a later king of the Catuvellauni, Cunebelin (Shakespeare's Cymbeline), who had increased his territory sufficiently to style himself King of Britain, used Latin lettering on his coins and cultivated good relations with the Emperors Augustus and Tiberius. During his reign the capital was moved from near St Albans to Colchester, and the beginnings of the growth of London started.

In A.D. 43 the Emperor Claudius sent his general Aulus Plautius on another invasion of Britain, and he followed in the same tracks as Caesar and crossed the Thames once again at Brentford. His crossing was easier than Caesar's, as the sight of an elephant among his troops proved too much for the British. Claudius took over command from Aulus and the Roman domination spread slowly across Britain.

Cunobelin was defeated and his new capital reduced, and the Romans turned westward. By A.D. 60 they were on the edge of the Welsh mountains when news of the uprising of Boadicea brought the legions hurrying southeastward. Boadicea wrought terrible vengeance on the Roman settlements, including London, only to be defeated with great slaughter in a battle, one possible site of which was near Hampstead Heath.

Britain remained under Roman domination for more than three hundred years longer, and what few remains we have show that Hendon had its Roman residents. The most important of these are those at Brockley Hill, Stanmore, at the point on Watling Street where the road bends to the right as it points towards St Albans. There are records of finds of Roman objects being made through the sixteenth, seventeenth and eighteenth centuries, including coins, urns and jewellery.

In 1937 systematic excavations began on this site, and these have continued. It has become apparent that here stood a prosperous Roman settlement with villas on the east side of the road and a large pottery on the west. The Roman name for this settlement was SULLONIACAE, which is a Latinized version of the old British name meaning the village or estate belonging to SUL, though we have no idea who this SUL was. When the Romans came in A.D. 43 they soon recognized the usefulness of the sandy clay on which the old British settlement was built. Forty years later their potteries were in full production, and for over a century these kilns produced tiles and all types of cheap crockery for the homes in the fast-growing Roman London.

During the second century the potteries began to decline, and by A.D. 200 the kilns were closed down and the area had been levelled and cleared for cultivation. No doubt the crops from these fields went to feed the residents in the houses across the road, for these were still being lived in. The Romans had built their own road, the road later known as Watling Street, and this settlement at Brockley Hill must have been an important stopping place on the road from London to St Albans. Some other Roman remains have also been found in Hendon, notably those at the Grove in the Burroughs, where tessellated pavement fragments have been found, so very possibly a Roman villa stood on this spot.

The end of Roman domination – the Dark Ages

For nearly four hundred years the Romans governed and lived in Britain. Many prominent British citizens adopted Roman dress, customs and religions. The land was surveyed and cultivated and the produce poured eastward towards the Roman provinces in Europe. On one occasion the Romans employed as many as eight hundred grain ships to keep their legions in Germany supplied, and a great deal of this grain came from the fields of Middlesex, so no doubt Hendon contributed its share. But the might of Rome was threatened at home by the encroachments of the Goths, and more and more troops were withdrawn from Britain to protect the homeland. Finally, in A.D. 410, the authorities in Rome warned the Britons that the last of the Roman troops were to be withdrawn and that they should be prepared to carry on their own defence against the Saxon invaders, who were already raiding the coasts of Britain.

With the final departure of the Romans a great darkness settles on the history of Britain, and little is known for certain about what went on during this period. The Angles and the Saxons raided and later invaded. They burned isolated Roman

Part of Dunstan's charter of A.D. 959 granting lands at Hendon to Westminster Abbey.

pasta ad pec' uille. Silua. xl. porc. 7 moliñ. de. v. sot.
h tra ualt. xxx. sot. 7 qdo recep. similit T.R.E. xl. sot.
hanc tra tenuit 7 tenet in dnio s petr Westmon.
In hund de Gare. ten Wills camerari sub abbe
s petri. ii. hid 7 dim in Chingesberie. Tra. ii. car.
In dnio. i. car. 7 uilli. i. car. Ibi. v. uilli. qsq; de. i. uirg.
7 i. cot. Silua. cc. porc. h tra ualt. xxx. sot. 7 qdo recep.
similit T.R.E. lx. sot. hanc tra tenuit Aluuin horne
teign regis. E. in uadimonio de qda hõe s petri.

Handone. ten abb s petri. p. xx. hid se defend.
Tra xvi. car. Ad dniu pain. x. hide. 7 ibi sunt. iii.
car. Uilli hnt. viii. car. 7 vi adhuc posf fieri. Ibi
pbr hñt. i. uirg. 7 iii. uilli qsq; dim h. 7 viii. uilli
qsq; i. uirg. 7 xxvi. uilli qsq; dim uirg. 7 xii. bord
q tenent dim hid. 7 vi. cot. 7 i. seru. ptã ii. bou.
Silua mille porc. 7 x. sot. In totis ualent ualt. viii.
lib. 7 qdo recep. similit T.R.E. xii. lib. hoc m
iacuit 7 iacet in dnio eccte s petri.

Hendon's entry in Domesday, 1086.

villas and laid waste their settlements, including the settlement at Brockley Hill. The Britons who were originally settled in the south-east were driven into Wales and the West country. But gradually these Anglo-Saxon invaders began to settle, and, although they had conquered the Britons they often fought amongst themselves, and the country was divided up into seven kingdoms. They brought their own pagan religions, and the new growth of Christianity that had come in the wake of the Romans was driven westwards and survived only in Wales. After the Saxons came the Danes, raiding far inland in their ships, and once again fighting spread across the kingdom, and no progress could be made. In A.D. 878 Alfred the Great, king of Wessex, in whose kingdom at this time Hendon was, defeated the Danes, so that they were glad to make peace. The treaty of Wedmore divided the country, so that the Danes kept one half and the Anglo-Saxons the other. For a short time the dividing line ran along the Watling Street, so that Hendon fell just within the Danelaw. We have no records of life in Hendon at this time, but the most significant happening in English history was the return of Christianity under Augustine at the end of the sixth century. When it reached Hendon we have no idea, but in a charter purporting to date from A.D. 959 the lands at Hendon were granted to the Monastery at Westminster by Dunstan, Archbishop of Canterbury. Dunstan claimed to have bought the land from King Edgar, and it is said to include land given even earlier by Kings Offa, Coenulph and Alfred. Later charters are said to confirm this grant by Edward the Martyr, and two further confirmations by Edward the Confessor were dated 1047 and 1066 just a few days before his death.

These charters are almost certainly copies made by the monks of Westminster at a later date who were anxious to convince William the Conqueror or his successors that their claim to the land was a good one.

FEUDAL HENDON

Hendon in Norman times – The Domesday survey

In 1066 Edward the Confessor, who was of the house of Alfred the Great, died. Edward had had great sympathy for the Norman way of life, and during his reign many Normans had been introduced into high places of Church and State. On his death the succession to the throne was not clear, and two chief claimants arose, Harold, son of Earl Godwin, and William of Normandy.

William invaded England in order to press his claim, and defeated Harold at Hastings. He was crowned king and England came under Norman domination. The old language, Anglo-Saxon, was replaced in higher society by Norman French and became despised as a peasant's tongue. During the next three hundred years this old language gradually absorbed much of the Norman language, just as the Norman invaders were absorbed into the population.

William was anxious that his new land should be carefully surveyed, so that he might know exactly how much he now owned. So in 1085 he held a great Council and set commissioners to find out how much land there was in each shire, how much belonged to the king and what dues he should receive annually, how much land was owned by the bishops, abbots and earls, and how much each landowner held in land and cattle, and the value of these. During the following year the survey was made, and Hendon's entry runs thus:

HANDONE, the Abbot of St Peter's, holds [the Manor of Hendon.] It was assessed for twenty hides. The arable land is sixteen carucates. Ten hides belong to the demesne and there are three ploughs there. The villeins have eight ploughs and five more could be made. A priest there has one virgate and three villeins have each half a hide; and seven villeins have each one virgate; and sixteen villeins have each half a virgate; and twelve bordars hold half a hide, and there are six cottars and one serf. There is a meadow for two oxen. Wood for a thousand pigs and ten shillings (rents). With all its profits it is worth eight pounds. When received it was the same. In the time of King Edward it was worth twelve pounds. This manor lay and lies in the demesne of the church of St Peter.

What can we tell about Hendon in 1086 from this document? First let us get the unfamiliar words out of the way. There are three terms of measurement: a virgate, which was about thirty acres, a hide which was four virgates (that is, about one hundred and twenty acres), and a carucate, which is the vaguest of the three and is often taken to mean an area of land as much as could be ploughed by one plough and a team of oxen in a year, and is obviously a very variable term, probably about one hundred acres. These terms of measurement are all rather uncertain and vary in different parts of the country, but the figures given above are those which are most usually taken as correct.

There are three different classes of society mentioned; a villein was a peasant occupier or cultivator who was subject to the lord, a bordar, who was a villein of the lower sort, and a cottar, who was a villein who held his land in return for service to the lord. It is not easy to distinguish these last two terms.

First then, the area of the manor is defined. It is confirmed that the Abbot of St Peter's, Westminster, is the lord of the manor; it makes an estimate at the value of the manor, making the point that it had declined in value since the time of King Edward, possibly because some of the inhabitants had been away fighting in the wars, and, consequently, the land had been neglected to some extent, and possibly because the Normans used more land for hunting than cultivation. It gives us some idea of the total population, 45 males are listed, giving an estimated total of about 200–250. It tells us that sufficient woodland for the feeding of a thousand pigs was available, which means that a great deal of Hendon was woodland. It mentions a priest, which tells us that a church must have existed, though it does not tell us where. Overall, it gives us a picture of an ordered society centred on the manor.

The other manor, Edgware, which, together with the manor of Hendon and other smaller sub-manors, makes up modern Hendon, does not appear by name in the Domesday book. It is first mentioned by name in a deed of A.D. 978 in its Anglo-Saxon form of Aegces wer. The first part of this name is probably a personal name, and the second part is Anglo-Saxon for a weir or fishing pool formed by a dam across a river.

Edgware is probably included in Domesday as part of the district called Stanmer, which is the Stanmore of today.

The origins of the manorial system are very obscure, and probably developed gradually over the preceding five hundred years until, by the time of Domesday, it was a normal unit of estate division and of local government. The counties were divided into hundreds (Hendon is in the Hundred of Gore), and the hundreds into manors.

Life in the manor was centred on the manor house. Where its original site was in Hendon we do not know, but it was probably near the church. Later on it was at Hendon Place, renamed in the nineteenth century Tenterden Hall, but, since the Abbot was lord of the manor at this time, it is more likely that it was within easy reach of the church. Not that the Abbot normally lived in Hendon. The priest who is mentioned in Domesday was supplied by the Abbey, and he may have lived in the manor house. The church probably stood where it stands now, for, if the old charters are to be believed and Hendon belonged to the Abbot in Anglo-Saxon times, it is quite possible that there was a church on the same site. Traces of the foundation of a Norman church have been discovered during the restoration of the parish church, and the splendid font dates to Norman times, although about a hundred years after Domesday.

The manor contained the demesne which was the lord's own land and the holdings of the villeins. The average holding of a villein was a virgate, which was about thirty acres, and the cottars' holdings were smaller.

The feudal system was based on the idea of service. The lord held his land from the king in return for service – the villein held his land from the lord in the same way. He had to plough some of the lord's land in spring and supply oxen for the winter ploughing or perform similar services. He was the lord's man and followed him in time of war. The lord administered justice in the manorial courts, and the villein was bound to accept its findings and to uphold the customs of the manor. The villein was tied to his land, and could not leave without his lord's permission. He had to pay dues to the lord when his land changed hands and sometimes on the marriage of his daughters. However, the lord depended on the villeins, so it was in his interest to treat them well. The common land of the manor was worked as one large farm by the joint efforts of the villeins. Their own holdings were strips of land in open fields, which were not divided by hedges but by strips of turf. As we can see from Hendon's Domesday entry, the woodland was used for the feeding of pigs, who ate the acorns and beech nuts beneath the trees, and cattle grazed on the common land. There would be a mill which belonged to the lord, for the use of which the villeins would have to pay. We do not know for certain where the mill was in Hendon at this time.

Sometimes the villeins were allowed to pay the lord money instead of service, but this custom came later and probably applied only to the more important of the tenants. The villeins' diet consisted largely of meat – probably a lot of pork – fruit, eggs and cheese. Bees were kept for their honey, used for sweetening in the absence of sugar. The produce of the land which was not needed for the use of the manor or the villeins was sold at the nearest market. The produce of the fields at Hendon went mainly to feed the monks in the monastery at Westminster.

By our standards the life of these twelfth century Hendonians was hard and primitive. Their houses were crude buildings of wattled timber, plastered over with a covering of clay and mud. Those that had upper stories would reach them by means of a ladder outside. Their furniture was crude and the floor was of stamped earth. But, although their life was hard, they were a sturdy and cheerful people. The manor was more or less self-supporting, and the exertions of their daily life left them with little time or energy to take much interest in social matters. Their society was a fixed one, and as long as they ate well they had little to complain of. The primitive sanitation and a diet lacking in green vegetables and fresh meat during the winter often led to sickness, and later to plague.

The pattern of life we see here continued with very little change through the next two hundred years, till, in 1348, the Black Death and the resultant disastrous drop in population saw the beginnings of a new era.

During this time the Abbots of Westminster remained lords of the manor, but they often granted it to others subject to an annual rent. In 1150 Gervase de Blois, the Abbot at that time, granted the manor of Hendon to Gilbert FitzGunter for an annual rental of £40. This Gervase did not manage the affairs of the Abbey very wisely, disposing of much of the Abbey lands to his friends and relations. Some of these were recovered by later Abbots, but others remained rented out until the dissolution of the monasteries.

The first mention of Edgware as a manor in its own right occurs in 1216, when the holding of the manor of Eggeswere, among others, was confirmed to the Countess of Salisbury.

Gilbert FitzGunter apparently disposed of his interest in the manor of Hendon to the family of de Rous, although there was an agreement in 1225 which suggests that the Abbot of Westminster still retained his interest in the manor.

In 1226 an action between Gilbert de Rous of Hendon and Abbot Richard of Barking was settled by Gilbert agreeing to pay an annual rental to the Abbot of £22, with thirty-six quarters of wheat, twenty quarters of meal and forty quarters of oats. He was also to provide men to work for the Abbot and to offer hospitality to him at Hendon each year for two days and part of a third. This agreement tells us something of the state in which the Abbot used to travel. Gilbert had to provide for the Abbot, his seven chief servants, and up to thirty followers. Thirty-five horses had to be fed and candles provided for the Abbot and his train. Each of the chief servants was to receive a shilling as he left Hendon. If the Abbot did not come in any one year Gilbert had to pay him ten marks.

Gilbert de Rous was one of Henry III's judges, and his family were staunch supporters of the king in his struggle with Simon de Montfort. A member of the de Rous family, Galfridus, who was sheriff of Beds. and Bucks. and lived at the manor house of Hendon, petitioned the king for recompense for damage done by John d'Egville and other barons, who were supporters of de Montfort in the recent war. Houses and corn were burnt – horses, arms and clothing were damaged, and money belonging to the king was stolen.

During the reign of Edward I in 1277 a survey of the manor of Edgware was included in an extent of the three manors of Shenley, Titehurst and 'Eggeswere and Kyngesbur' (Edgware and Kingsbury). In this extent the area of the demesne lands is described and divided up into garden, grove, meadowland and arable land, and their respective values set out. Then the tenants and their holdings are listed. Included in these are the Knights of St John of Jerusalem, whose land was worth 7s 7d per year. This was the estate later known as Edgware Woods or Edgware Boys (Bois), which became a sub-manor.

Typical of the entries of the customary tenants is:

'Richard atte Graue holds half a virgate of land for 2s 11½d. And he owes in autumn four men to reap, of whom three are at the lord's food, and the works are worth 4d. And he owes one man for two days before dinner to bind, and the work is worth 1d. And he owes two men to reap and is worth 1d. And he ought to harrow for one day before dinner, and the work is worth three halfpence. And he ought to hedge for one day before dinner, and the work is worth a halfpenny. And he ought to carry before dinner at the lord's food for one day, and the work is worth three halfpence.

<blockquote>
Sum of the rent 2s 11½d
Sum of the value of the work .. .. 9½d'
</blockquote>

At the end of the extent are set out the common duties of all the customary tenants, thus:

'Memorandum that all the aforesaid customary tenants ought to mow the whole of the above said meadow, to toss (the hay) to carry (it), and to make the haycocks at their own charge in the lord's court. And they shall have from the lord 6d and one cheese, price 2d, and salt or ½d. And the work is worth over and above 6s 0d.'

The manor of Edgware was held at this time by Adam de Stratton from the Priory of St Bartholomew, Smithfield. Adam de Stratton was an unparalleled rogue even by mediaeval standards. Under the patronage of the Countess of Albemarle he held office in the exchequer, where, with the help of his three brothers, he carried on a career of extortion, forgery and malpractice that eventually led to his ruin. His activities received some measure of royal protection, for as long as the money continued to pour into the royal coffers little attention was paid to the methods used in obtaining it. In 1279 Adam was dismissed from his offices and convicted of fraud and forgery, yet, despite this, he managed to reinstate himself, until in 1289 and 1290 further scandalous malpractices led to his final disgrace. Even after this there is rumour that he was employed on secret royal business, even to the extent of tampering with the will of his patroness, the Countess of Albemarle.

In 1312 Richard de Rous of Hendon came to an agreement with the Abbot of Westminster, whereby he exchanged the manor of Hendon for the neighbouring manor of Hodford, lying just to the south. This manor had come into the possession of the Abbot as a present from the King, Edward I, in return for prayers said for the soul of his Queen, Eleanor, who died in 1298.

If the Abbot did travel from Westminster to his country manor at Hendon with his formidable train the road he travelled was not the metalled highway we know today, nor even the paved highway of the Romans. After the Romans left and the collapse of central government, the road system they had built up began to decline. It was nobody's responsibility in the Dark Ages to maintain the roads, and they soon fell into disuse, so that traffic between towns nearly ceased. In feudal times the upkeep and the administration of the highways within the manor was the responsibility of the lord of the manor, and was enforced on him by law. The lord in his turn would distribute this responsibility on his tenants, and this he enforced in the manorial courts. This is in contrast to Roman times, when a central body was responsible for the roads; the responsibility was now local, and this continued up to the twentieth century, at the present time being shared between the control of the Ministry of Transport and the various local authorities.

The road the Abbot's horses trod then was just a part of the land set aside for the passage of travellers, which in time became a trodden track. Because of the necessity for avoiding the tilled land, and because of the natural tendency for travellers to avoid steep hills, the road would wander along, unlike the arrow-straight Roman roads. Watling Street, although no physical trace of the Roman road remained, was still in use, and it is interesting to note as early as 1315 a toll was imposed on travellers to help to pay for upkeep of the road and a citizen of Edgware was appointed to collect the tolls. But the route from

Hendon to Westminster lay along a different way, running probably along what is now North End Road to Hampstead (the manor of which also belonged to Westminster), via Chalk Farm, St Giles, Charing to Westminster. Other fourteenth century roads in Hendon would have been less important, but early maps refer to what we now know as Colindeep Lane as Ancient Street, so we must presume a well-trodden way of early standing. Parson Street, near the vicarage, was also mentioned by name in the early fourteenth century, and still exists today.

Equally a responsibility of the lord to maintain were the bridges, and Hendon, with its many streams, has frequent mentions of this activity in its early documents, both in the manorial courts and as indictments of the lord by the law of the land.

The Survey of 1321

We have set the scene now for the Survey of Hendon made in 1321. Firstly, why was this survey made? The country had settled now into a time of comparative peace – the Norman invaders had been more or less absorbed into the native population and a balance of power had been reached between king and barons. The lords of the manor probably felt that the time was ripe for a stocktaking. In 1312 a survey was made of the neighbouring manor of Hampstead, and in 1321 it was the turn of Hendon. Reflected in this document we can see the development of Hendon since Domesday. In 1321 there were now fifty-one free tenants – that is, paying rental only – and seventy-five customary – that is, tenants who still paid at least part of their rental in the form of service to the lord. The tenants seem prosperous enough, and the idea of common tillage seems to be disappearing, so that each tenant held his own portion of land, working it sometimes with the help of paid labour. The large amount of woodland available in Hendon gave opportunity for fresh land to be cleared and cultivated, and men who could learn a trade could work as free labourers for the lord or for other tenants. Indeed, these newer class of paid labourers were often better off than the old customary tenants, although the difference was not so marked in Hendon as it was elsewhere. This prosperity is all the more noteworthy because the period just before 1321 had been marked by poor harvests and high prices.

The various officials who worked for the manor are set out in this survey, and those tenants who were liable to take such offices are mentioned. The bailiff who was appointed by the lord to look after his interest, and the reeve who was elected by the villeins to accept responsibility for them. Between them these two men would see that all the customary tenants performed their due services. There was normally a hayward, who was responsible for the corn, the meadows and the seeds, and to take charge of straying cattle. The shepherd was also important, and in Hendon, with all its large herds of swine, the swineherd would have been especially busy. The simple mechanisms in use on the land, and the needs of the horses, would receive attention from the smith and the carpenter. Life was not all work, and the lord had to provide feasts on certain days for all the tenants and their wives. The lord had two gardens of considerable size, producing fruit and herbs, and tenants who were not required on the land could work their service there. The lord of the manor owned a mill, and, although its position is not stated, its place in the survey would make us believe it to be near the church, which would be convenient for the lord of the manor, who lived nearby, and the top of a hill would be a likely place. Some of the freeholders were important men. Sir Henry Scrope, who held the manor of Hodford, held land in Hendon; Henry of Bydick, who was an M.P. for Middlesex, was a tenant paying an annual rent of 7s 10d and a pair of gilt spurs worth sixpence. Women could be tenants in their own right, although this usually came about as an inheritance from a dead husband. The hospitals of St James and of St John also held land in Hendon.

The Black Death

This then was a picture of Hendon at the height of the feudal system, for in 1348 the disastrous effects of the Black Death and all its subsequent disorders were the beginning of the end of the old order. It is estimated that from a third to a half of the population of England perished in less than two years, and this drastic cut in the available labour obviously strengthened the villeins' position. Instead of a shortage of land, which had been growing during the gradual increase of population, there was now a shortage of men to till it. The value of farms fell, and at the same time the cost of labour rose. Many of the lord's tenants died and their holdings returned to the lord, who could no longer afford to farm them. A new class of yeoman farmers began to grow through the amalgamation of these smaller holdings, and these farmers had necessarily to depend on paid labour. They rebelled against the continuance of the various servile dues and services previously expected of them, and the lord was forced to commute these services for cash. As the lord could no longer afford to farm the demesne himself he often let this, either in return for money rents or for produce to fill his own table. This new class of yeoman farmers were to be the backbone of England's economy for the next two hundred years. Hendon was less affected by the Black Death than some other manors. Since it had always belonged to the Abbot of Westminster, there was not the same relation between lord and tenant as there was in some manors. The customary tenants at the time of the 1321 Survey were expected to do far less service than was usual, so that the economic upsets that followed the Black Death made little mark.

The Peasants' Revolt

The gap that existed between lord and villein was disappearing; the villein was now either a yeoman farmer or a landless labourer, and disputes were soon evident between these two divisions of the peasantry. The new small farmers, with the support of the lords, tried to reassert the old wages that prevailed before the Black Death, and the labourers joined together to combat these attempts. All this unrest finally culminated in the rising of 1381 which was put down in the reign of Richard II. This rising, which is associated with the name of Wat Tyler and Jack Straw, was set in motion by the poll taxes that were levied in an attempt to raise money to pay for the war in France.

Locally this rising does not seem to have caused much trouble, but in Barnet and Harrow there were serious outbreaks. The people of St Albans, in common with many villages near London, marched on London, and they probably passed through Hendon on their way. Some inhabitants of Hendon were involved in the troubles, however, for two of them were specifically excluded from the amnesty that was granted after the troubles were over. These two were John Knot de Childeshill and John in the Hale, but they were both acquitted by jury in 1386.

Hendon was one of those manors where the freeholds were bought up and let on lease, and the same was done with the demesne lands. We have records of succeeding farmers of the demesne and the collectors of rents, and, later, of stewards of the manor.

The Manorial courts

Before we move on to discuss the fifteenth century in Hendon it seems an appropriate moment to give an account of the manorial courts that have been mentioned before.

The stewards of the manor were responsible for the holding of the courts of the manor, and these were generally held twice a year. The steward considered there all questions of rents, markets, mills and holdings of land. He was the president of the court, the bailiff was the lord's representative and, when necessary, prosecutor. The tenants of the manor attended the court and gave judgment. The steward settled the procedure and gave the final sentence. Attendance at the courts was compulsory. The courts could deal with petty criminal offences, such as small thefts, but in the main dealt with offences against the customs of the manor, such as bad ploughing and improper taking of wood from the lord's land. The court appointed the manorial officers, such as the constables, but its most important duty was in recording the transfer of land holdings within the manor. The procedure was for the outgoing tenant to surrender the land to the court, and then the purchaser was admitted to the land by the court. The manor courts were divided into two sections, Court Leet and Court Baron. The Court Leet dealt with offences of the tenants, and Court Baron with the tenants and their holdings. Courts were normally held at the manor house, but in later years at Hendon they were held at the White Bear.

Richard II had received the sub-manors of Hodford and Cowhouse from Sir Richard le Scrope, who surrendered them to Richard in 1399 in exchange for lands in Yorkshire. Richard granted them to the Abbot of Westminster in return for prayers for his soul and for that of his late Queen, Anne. The holdings of the Abbey of Westminster in Hendon were thus consolidated by these two neighbouring sub-manors.

In 1399 Richard II was deposed and succeeded by Henry IV, who reigned till 1413, when he was succeeded by Henry V. Henry was soon involved in a war with France, and a great deal of the money for the waging of this war was found by the church. The Archbishop of Canterbury was responsible for this, but in later years he repented of his support for a war that caused so many deaths, so that, when he died, he left money to found a college at Oxford to pray for the souls of those who had fallen. This college, All Souls, Oxford, was endowed with lands in Hendon and Edgware which they still hold to this day.

In 1455 the Wars of the Roses broke out, and Hendon, being so near to London, must have felt some of the upheaval of this struggle for power between York and Lancaster.

In the first year of the war a battle was fought just outside St Albans, and Henry VI was wounded and captured by the Yorkists. The captive king was led from St Albans to London, and it is likely that the triumphant procession led through Hendon. After following the Watling Street south as far as Hendon, the easiest way would branch off at Colindeep Lane and lead through Hendon over Hampstead and so to London. Certainly this road was an important one, as, just before this date, the Abbot was indicted as the responsible lord of the manor for not keeping this highway in repair. In 1461 another battle was fought at St Albans, and this time the Yorkists were defeated and fled in rout to London. This panic-stricken flight, so different from the triumphant procession of six years before, would have passed through Hendon either by the same route as before or by Watling Street to Hyde Park Corner, or by the hilly route from Boreham Wood, Highwood Hill and Mill Hill. After this battle London declared for York and chose Edward, Earl of March, as their king, Edward IV. The court rolls of the manor begin in proper sequence in 1461, and we find in them many of the family names that persist in Hendon records for many hundreds of years. Names of families that have grown into this new class of yeoman farmers, families like the Nicolls, Marshes, Kemps and the Brents.

Another decisive battle in the Wars of the Roses was fought only just outside the northern boundaries of Hendon at Barnet in 1471, and the armies marching to and from the battle must have passed through Hendon.

TUDORS AND STUARTS

Tudor Hendon

The ending of the Wars of the Roses with the battle of Bosworth in 1485 saw the accession of the House of Tudor. Henry VII, the first of that line, played little part in the history of Hendon, but when his son, Henry VIII, came to the throne there were to be events of vital interest to Hendon. Henry's first great minister was Cardinal Wolsey, who aspired to the Papacy but who in fact led England towards the split with Rome and the setting up of the Reformed Church of England. Wolsey held the Abbey of St Albans, at that time the most powerful in England, but in 1529 he was dismissed by Henry and later appointed to the Archbishopric of York. In the spring of 1530 Wolsey left his palace at Richmond on his way to York, where he intended to spend his last days. He stayed at the Abbots Bower, Hendon Place, which was the manor house, and, having equipped his servants in livery suitable to his state, set out for York. His way lay down an avenue of yew trees following the line of Tenterden Grove, crossing over Parson Street along the bridle path of Ashley Lane. Thence his path lay along the Ridgeway, up Highwood Hill, onto the Elstree Road and forward to the Abbey of St Albans.

Henry's first wife, Katherine of Aragon, whom he divorced in favour of Anne Boleyn, died possessed of lands in Hendon, though they do not seem to have lain within the manor itself.

In 1539 Henry's policy finally culminated in the Dissolution of the Monasteries and the forfeit of all their lands to the king.

Copt Hall, Mill Hill, the home of the Nicoll family for centuries, now demolished.

Hendon House, Brent Street, home of John Norden the Elizabethan cartographer, now demolished.

In 1540 the Abbot of Westminster resigned, and Henry created a new Bishopric of Westminster, with Middlesex for its diocese. This new bishopric was endowed with the lands and properties of the suppressed Monastery of Westminster, and Hendon was, of course, among these. The new Bishop was Bishop Thirleby and Hendon was part of the endowment granted by letters patent in 1542. Thirleby was not a good manager, and he disposed of nearly all the property until in 1550 it was reduced to a deanery. In that year Hendon was surrendered to the Crown.

The young King Edward VI, in return for good and faithful services, granted the Manor of Hendon to Sir William Herbert. In return Sir William was to pay 'a service of one fortieth part of a knight's fee for all services and demands.'

Sir William, by now Earl of Pembroke, gave the Manor of Hendon as a wedding present to his second son, Edward, on his marriage in 1569.

Shortly after this marriage certain of the customary tenants were ordered to draw up a survey of the Manor of Hendon. This survey took nearly two years to complete (1574–1576), and just before it was finished a lawsuit confirmed the conveyance of the manor to Sir Edward and his heirs for ever. The survey was presented in October, 1576. In its introduction the names of the customary tenants who carried out the survey are set out. From the twenty-four names six are of the Nicoll family, six of the Marsh family, and we note that the order to carry out the survey was given at a Manorial court. Next the boundaries of the manor are set out, and these are followed by an enumeration of the 'ancient customs' used in the said Manor of Hendon. These confirm the rights and the duties of both the lord and the tenants. Among these were the lord's right to a year's rent for any copyhold that changed at the death of a tenant, and the right of the tenant to cut the timber growing on his land. Twelve of these ancient customs are listed. Then follow the names, holdings, rents and services due of the copyhold tenants. Typical of these is:

c

'WILLIAM MARSH holdeth one tenement called Slattans and renteth yearly to the lord ....ii^{s}vi^d
For service ....ix^{s}viii^d
and tenn bushells of otes'

From this we see one of the largest families in the Manor, one of its holdings is named and its money rent set out. We can see that the customary service due to the lord was commuted for money, and the amount of produce also due to the lord is set out. After the copyhold tenants come the freehold tenants, who are treated in the same manner.

Elizabethan Hendon

In 1521 an Act of Parliament had been passed making it compulsory for every male over fourteen to have a bow and two shafts. One Hendon resident was found guilty of neglecting to do this in 1561. The same Act stated that each district should set up butts for archery practice, but Hendon failed to do this until 1597, when the constable was specifically ordered to do so.

Henry VIII's illustrious daughter, Elizabeth I, travelled about her country a great deal, and she paid several visits to Hendon Place, once the country house of the Abbots of Westminster, now the residence of the Herberts. Sir Edward's father, the Earl of Pembroke, was Elizabeth's Lord High Steward, and was one of the persons appointed to carry out the terms of Henry's will. The Earl seemed to have played his cards carefully, as he was rewarded both by Catholic Queen Mary and Protestant King Edward.

Sir Edward Herbert later let his house at Hendon to Sir John Fortescue. Sir John was a Privy Councillor to Elizabeth and used Hendon Place as a country residence. Elizabeth paid another visit to Hendon during his tenancy.

Living in Hendon at this time was John Norden, famous antiquary and cartographer. He lived in Hendon House in Brent Street, on a site now occupied by the Hendon County School.

In 1595 Sir Edward Herbert died and his son William

succeeded to the title and to the lordship of the Manor of Hendon. He confirmed the tenancy of Hendon Place to Fortescue.

During Elizabeth's reign it is interesting to note several occasions in which Hendon residents figured in the Middlesex Session Rolls. One unfortunate lady, a servant of John Naylor, was whipped and burnt on the left ear for leaving the service of her master. Another resident, Robert Chandler, was fatally wounded in a brawl with Edward Edwardes, and, despite the fact that Chandler did not die for another four months, Edwardes was condemned to death. Elizabeth's reign was notable for various acts passed concerned with good local government, regulating, among other things, the taking-in of lodgers and the prevention of vagrants from becoming a burden on the parish. Perhaps the greatest of these Acts was the Poor Relief Act of 1601. In mediaeval times the duty of relieving the poor, though falling legally on the manor, was more often carried by the church. Of course, before the Dissolution the monasteries themselves did a great deal of useful charitable work, but by the beginning of the sixteenth century their funds were no longer sufficient for the task, and it became necessary for the State to take action against the hordes of beggars and vagabonds roaming the countryside. With the suppression of the monasteries a new poor law was found necessary, and the duty of caring for their own poor was given to each individual parish. Indeed, by an Act passed in 1536, the private giving of alms was made punishable by a fine of ten times the amount given.

The Act of 1601 was the foundation of poor law administration for the next two hundred years. It ordered the churchwardens and other substantial parishioners to be appointed as overseers of the poor, whose duty it was to maintain and set to work the poor of the parish.

The gradual development of the parish had its beginnings even earlier than that of the manor, and they existed side by side for many centuries. The division of the various duties of local government between the two authorities varies from place to place, and probably Hendon, being an ecclesiastical manor, would have felt the division less than other manors. But after the Dissolution the churchwardens must have assumed some of the duties previously carried out by the Abbot's representative, and that of the relief of the poor would have been the most appropriate. The governing body of the parish was the vestry, who would elect churchwardens, and the part they played in local government steadily increases as that of the manor decreases. In Hendon the vestry met in the Greyhound Inn, formerly called Church House, although the first reference to it by name does not appear till 1655. The rent from the Greyhound was applied in the reduction of the poor rate which the vestry levied.

Stuart Hendon

In 1603 Hendon received another royal visit. This time it was James I who stayed as the guest of Sir John Fortescue at Hendon Place. During his visit he knighted two gentlemen, William Fleetwood of Bucks. and Thomas Hesketh of Lancashire.

Sir William Herbert, the new lord of the manor, married the daughter of the Earl of Northumberland, Eleanor Percy, and was created Baron Powis in the same year, 1629.

Another prominent resident at this time was Lord Chief Justice Crewe, who was later dismissed because he refused to admit the legality of forced loans. He was defended in Parliament by another Hendon resident, Denzil Hollis.

In 1632 Percy, the son of Sir William Herbert, was knighted and created baronet in the same year. At this time his father handed the Manor of Hendon over to him, and the survey of the manor that was made (1632–35) seems to have been carried out in connection with this handing over.

The survey of 1632–35 follows the same pattern as previous surveys; the names of the customary tenants making the presentment are listed. Nicolls and Marshes, names which soon become familiar in a study of Hendon's old documents, are prominent. The boundaries, unchanged since the last survey, are set out, together with the ancient customs of the manor. Then follows a list of the copyhold tenants and their holdings, rents and dues, and, lastly, the freehold tenants and their holdings. An interesting item among these is a tenant who paid only a red rose at midsummer to the lord of the manor in return for his holding.

Another function that the parish in the form of the vestry took over gradually from the manor was that of maintenance of the roads. The first Act of Parliament that really attempted to apportion the responsibility for road maintenance was passed in 1555. The duty of the parish under this act was to nominate from the parishioners a surveyor (sometimes more than one) of highways or waywarden. All the tools, cartage and labour he required had to be provided free by the parishioners. All this labour and material was used at the direction of the surveyor. From 1691 the appointment of the surveyor was confirmed by the local Justices of the Peace at special highways sessions. The post of surveyor was not a popular one for obvious reasons, and, consequently, it was served in turn by the parishioners. He rendered his accounts to the J.Ps. and they authorized the raising of a highway rate.

The accounts of the Hendon surveyors begin in 1703. The district was divided into north and south ends, with a surveyor for each, but a year later an additional one for each end was appointed. We can see from the accounts that most of the materials were gathered locally, the gravel coming from Hampstead, Brent Street, Mill Hill and Stanmore. The origin of this gravel is referred to in the opening remarks on the geology of Hendon and district.

Copt Hall, Mill Hill, the home of one branch of the Nicoll family, was probably built by Randall Nicoll in 1624 as a beam bearing that date was found at Copt Hall at the time of the demolition, although this beam may originally have come from another Nicoll home – Cookes.

The Civil War

The middle years of the seventeenth century saw England torn by the Civil War. The Herberts, by tradition and religion, were supporters of the Crown's cause, but Hendon itself, due to its proximity to London, as well as the inclinations of its inhabitants, in the main supported the Parliament.

In 1644, after a spirited defence, the Powis Castle in Montgomeryshire was stormed by the Parliament forces and Lord Powis sent prisoner to London, where, however, he was allowed to live on parole in his own lodgings. The Manor of Hendon had been sequestered because of the support given to the king by Sir Percy Herbert, lord of the manor. These activities included raising trained bands in Montgomery and collecting money in this country for use in Charles I's war in Scotland. Sir Percy was arrested in 1641 after being summoned to attend a committee of Parliament. He was compelled to swear allegiance to Parliament and then released on bail. In 1650 he was punished by a heavy fine for his part in the defence of Powis Castle, and his estates, including Hendon, were sequestered and sold. However, the Manor of Hendon was let to relatives of Sir Percy's wife, Elizabeth Craven, for we find John Craven and William Gibson as lords of the manor in 1649, and in 1650 Sir William Craven and two other gentlemen were admitted as tenants. The commissioners appointed by Parliament had possession of the manor during the Commonwealth, and they were responsible for the lettings. During this period various tenants with free and copyhold holdings made complaint that the county committee administering the manor were extorting more than the customary dues from them. But more important from the point of view of local history is the fact that, during the Commonwealth, an act was passed in 1653 ordering that the parish should keep a register of births, marriages and deaths. From the next year the registers in Hendon begin. Sir Percy's father died in 1655 and was buried in the parish church. Sir Percy himself had lost all his money and estates, and his son William was imprisoned in the Tower in 1659 on suspicion of plotting against the Commonwealth.

With the Restoration in 1660 Hendon returned to the Herberts, and the new lord of the manor was William, who was later created marquis and then Duke of Powis by James II. He had let the manor in 1680 to a Mr Samuel Turner for £400 a year. During the reign of the restored Charles II another resident of Hendon was involved in a dramatic incident.

In 1678 Titus Oates' Popish plot had inflamed a people already suspicious of Charles II and his Catholic leanings. Lord William Russell, then living at Highwood House, Mill Hill, was a prominent Whig, which party took a lead in forcing through the Exclusion Bill. The Whigs did little to calm the uproar, and used it to party advantage, even to the extent of plotting with Monmouth. The Tory-Royalist party, despite the efforts of moderates on both sides, finally reacted when the Rye House plot to kill the king and his brother was exposed and the Whigs were scattered. Shaftesbury, their leader, died in exile, and Russell and others were to die on the scaffold. (Local legend has it that in 1681 the order was issued to arrest Russell at Highwood and King's Messengers were sent to Mill Hill. Despite a desperate attempt to escape through a small window he was captured, brought to London and imprisoned in the Tower.) In fact, he appears to have been arrested at his London home. He faced his trial with great courage and stood by his principles steadfastly. He was beheaded in Lincoln's Inn Fields in 1683, and his body was temporarily buried at Highwood. Later it was removed to the family vault of the Bedford family at Chenies, Bucks.

William, Lord Marquis of Powis, lord of the manor, was a staunch supporter of James II and fled with his royal master in 1688 to France. For this he was made outlaw and his lands and titles forfeited to the Crown. His son, Lord Montgomery, did not go with him, and seems to have made his peace with the new

sovereigns. The estates of his father were not, however, immediately returned to him, and the Crown continued to receive
the revenues of the Manor of Hendon.

In 1693 Lord Montgomery petitioned to have the Hendon
estates leased to him at a rent of £770 per year. The Treasury
referred the petition to the Receivers for Middlesex, who made
conflicting replies. One stated that the Crown would lose by
letting at that rent, and that the tenants already in possession of
holdings within the manor feared that new leases would not be
granted to them by a new lord of the manor, and that, anyway,
the position of Hendon so near to London made it necessary for
it not to be held by anyone whose attitude to the Crown was in
any way suspect. The other report stated that the offer was a
fair one, and that the tenants might be granted new leases by
the Crown before the transfer. Faced with these conflicting
reports the Treasury hesitated, and in 1696 the lordship of the
manor was granted to the Earl of Rochford. This grant caused
the Lord Montgomery to make a fresh protest, and on this
occasion he was able to show that the manor had been settled on
his mother by his father before the marquis was made outlaw.
The manor was thus restored to the marchioness, and later to
Lord Montgomery.

In following thus the story of the lordship of the manor down
to the end of the seventeenth century we have gone a little ahead
of the story of Hendon in general.

In 1688 the Kemp family re-built their house near the parish
church. This is the house we now know as Church Farm House
Museum, and this has been carefully restored and set out as a
museum of local history by the Hendon Borough Council. The
most striking feature from the outside is the massive central
chimney stack, and once inside the door we find that the central
passage actually runs through this stack. Some of the panelling
has been preserved, and the kitchen has been furnished with
equipment typical of the seventeenth-eighteenth centuries. In
the other rooms are displayed items, prints and documents of

local interest, and a general view of the history of Hendon may be had by making a tour through its rooms. This was probably the house attached to the manorial farm; hence its name and the name of the road that used to run by it, Hall Lane (now Greyhound Hill).

Between 1660-1677, living at Hendon House, Norden's old house in Brent Street, was Sir Jeremy Whichcot. During the period of the Commonwealth he had purchased the post of the Warden of the Fleet Prison, and through this office he was able to give some measure of comfort to imprisoned supporters of the king. After his death Hendon House remained in the Whichcot family till 1691.

If the flight of James II brought about an eclipse in the fortunes of the Herbert family, it did little to impair the career of another Hendon resident, Sir William Rawlinson. Rawlinson was created Sergeant-at-Law by James II in 1686. He was appointed a Commissioner of the Great Seal by William and Mary in 1689. It was he who purchased Hendon House from the Whichcots in 1691.

Both Rawlinson and Sir Jeremy Whichcot are buried in the parish church at Hendon. One of Rawlinson's daughters married John Aislabie, who had taken the manor house, Hendon Place, on lease. Aislabie had a brilliant career, serving as a lord of the Admiralty, Privy Councillor and Chancellor of the Exchequer. He suffered a great downfall later, when he was involved in the affair of the South Sea Bubble of 1721.

Hendon residents through the ages have been prepared to suffer for their religious beliefs. The Herberts, as we have seen, for their Catholicism and others for their Nonconformist beliefs. During the Commonwealth, Puritan ministers were intruded into the parish churches. At Hendon, Francis Warham, appointed as minister in 1643, was well liked by his parishioners till at the Restoration he was turned out of the living. He retired to Mill Hill. Richard Swift served in the same capacity at Edgware till the Act of Uniformity passed after the Restoration saw him deprived of his living. Like Warham, he retired to Mill Hill, and there started a school. Despite many difficulties, including more than one imprisonment in Newgate for practising his religious beliefs, he was well thought of in the district. During this time a Friends Meeting was established at Rosebank, Mill Hill Village, a house which still stands, in association with another at Gutter-shedge in the southern part of Hendon. The meeting apparently prospered, and was often visited by George Fox, the founder of the Quakers.

In 1674 Edward Kemp, a member of another numerous and long-standing Hendon family, was serving his turn as parish constable. The northern approaches to London were plagued by highwaymen, and, on hearing that a band of these rogues were escaping across country towards Hampstead, Kemp raised a body of horsemen from the neighbourhood and strove to cut the robbers off by striking down the Edgware Road. In the ensuing struggle Kemp and another resident of Hendon were killed.

THE EIGHTEENTH CENTURY

Poor Relief in the early eighteenth century

At the time of the Great Fire in London, funds, collected in the parish church, were sent to the Lord Mayor for the relief of the suffering and homeless.

In this age of the Welfare State, when every aspect of our health and welfare is catered for by the State agencies, we sometimes forget that in the days before the Industrial Revolution, before our population increased in size and became coagulated in the manufacturing towns, health and welfare were at one time the responsibility of the parish, and that what is now done through an impersonal official source was then an act of service performed on a neighbourly basis.

Just how complete the coverage of this parish service was we can gather by examining a typical entry in the Overseers of the Poor's account books. The year is 1703. First are set out the assessments of the south end of the parish, listing the amounts due from each householder who was liable. These amounts, together with the amount carried forward from the previous period and the amounts of tithes and royalties, amounted to £158 9s 1d. Next, the way in which this money was spent was set out, and we can see the amazing variety of ways in which it was expended.

Typical entries are such as these:

Gave Rich. Darnels wife relief in her sickness £1. 15s. 0d.
Pd. for Joseph Castle's girl 52 weeks   £5.   4s. 0d.
   (presumably an orphan cared for by the parish)

Gave Goody Nicol to by (buy) her son a pair of stockings	1s. 0d.
Pd. for the mending of Castle's girl's shooves (shoes)	10d.
Pd. Wm. Gardner for maimed soldiers and mariners	£1. 1s. 8d.
Pd. Wm. Gardner for a poor woman that lodged and died at his house	10s. 0d.
Pd. for her cofin	6s. 0d.
Pd. for her burial	8s. 0d.
Pd. a quarter's rent for Widow Marshal	5s. 0d.

These are just taken at random.

Then follows a similar assessment and expenditure for the north end of the parish. A sequence of items here tells a story of domestic tragedy and simple aid.

Pd. for Mordecai Hall's child, two months ..	£1. 0s. 0d.
Pd. for a cofin and shroud and bread and cheese and beer, and an affidavit	8s. 6d.
Pd. to Shepherd for the death	4s. 0d.
for faggots for Hall's wife	7s. 6d.
for relief at several times in her lying-in	£1. 15s. 0d.
Pd. for nursing another child of Hall's	12s. 0d.
Pd. for the burial of Hall's child	6s. 0d.
Gave Hall's wife more relief at times	£1. 10s. 6d.
Pd. for wood for Hall's wife	3s. 0d.
Pd. tho: Shepherd for the birth of Hall's child	2s. 0d.

Another duty of the parish was the putting out to apprenticeship the children in the care of the parish, and we find several entries of this sort:

Expended in binding Sarah Castle, apprentice	£1. 3s. 0d.

Another series of entries in another year reads:

Gave Widow Murrin relief	2s. 6d.
Expended to get Saml. Murrin into Bedlam	6s. 0d.
Expended in going after Saml. Murrin	5s. 0d.
Expended in having him to London	5s. 0d.

Expended in looking after him	7s.	6d.
Gave Goody Murrin to have her husband cryed	1s.	0d.
Gave him relief	5s.	0d.
Expended in having him to the doctors	£1. 7s.	0d.
Expended in going to the Lord Mayor and the chief officer of Bedlam about Saml. Murrin	1. 0s.	0d.

Edgware and Hendon – changes at the mid-eighteenth century

About this time, just beyond the north-western boundary of the parish of Edgware, there was a great deal of activity, as James Brydges, Duke of Buckingham and Chandos, was building his great mansion at Canons Park. He also rebuilt St Lawrence (Whitchurch), and it was in this church that Handel, Master of Music to the Duke, played. The Duke was another who lost a fortune in the South Sea Bubble, and Canons Park was pulled down in 1747 by his son Henry, the second Duke, and the materials dispersed. The great columns of the portico of Hendon Hall are said to be those originally at Canons.

Mention of Hendon Hall brings us to the next change in holding of the lordship of the Manor of Hendon. William, the last Marquis of Powis, died without issue in 1748, and a few years later the manor was sold by auction by direction of the executors of the late marquis in 1756. It was purchased by a Mr Clutterbuck for the great actor David Garrick, who paid the sum of £13,381 for the lordship and the right to present the living of St Mary's. At the same time he built a new house for himself, Hendon Hall (now Hendon Hall Hotel) although no records exist of him actually living there. The demesne lands were sold off to various purchases for a total of £40,580.

The eighteenth century

This point, midway through the eighteenth century, is a good moment to pause and take stock of the condition of Hendon at this time and to reflect on the changes that had taken place since the time of the Domesday survey. It was noted that in Norman times the greater part of the manor was taken up by forest land capable of supporting 1,000 pigs. In a survey of agriculture in Middlesex made towards the end of the eighteenth century Hendon's entry is as follows:

	Number of A R P	No. Houses	No. Inhab.	No. of Baptisms	No. of Burials	Waste Land
Hendon	8204 – –	240	–	46,4	58,1	–

	Nurseries	Arable	Grass	Mark. Gard.
	–	300	7,700	–

About 120 acres of woodland; the soil, mostly clay, with a mixture of gravel.

It can be seen that with the exception of some 120 acres of woodland, the whole of the parish has been cleared and that for the most part is it meadow with just a small percentage of arable land. The population about this time was approximately 1,900, almost all of whom were engaged in agriculture. With the exception of the clearing of the woodland, however, change had been small. Most of the roads and trackways had existed for centuries and most of the families living here had done so for centuries.

The sale of the Manor of Hendon by the last of that line of the Herbert family that had held the manor since the Dissolution of the Monasteries was an event signalling the close of an era. Its purchase in 1756 by David Garrick, actor-manager and man-about-town marks the beginning of the new Hendon. From this moment on the rate of change begins to accelerate. In the years to come, especially as the means of communication with London improved, an increasing number of estates in Hendon were purchased by families who had their livelihood in London and who saw in rural Hendon a convenient relief from crowded town or by people who came to Hendon for peace and seclusion in their retirement.

It was at this time that the gradual decay of the farmhouse and its replacement by the villa began. This process would continue well into the twentieth century but its progress was inexorable. Because many of these 'new' Hendonians took happily to rural pursuits and worked their estates as small farms, the apparent change was at first very small so that comparison of Crow's map of 1754 and Cooke's map of 1796 shows but little alteration. The most important addition had been that of Hendon Hall built by Garrick to be his manor house but apparently not used by him. Other large houses occupied at this time (1796) were Copt Hall (Nicoll), Hendon Place (Snow), Manor House, Golders Hill (Bond), Highwood House (Brown), Hendon House, Brent Street (Cornwall).

THE NINETEENTH CENTURY

The New Roads

The building of new roads and improvements in the old accelerated the rate of change and as the estates grew smaller the dawning of the day of the speculative builder grew nearer. By the time that Francis Whishaw's map of 1828 was drawn, the first scar on Hendon's landscape, the Finchley Road, had been drawn. This road had been established by Act of Parliament in 1826 and ran from St John's Chapel near Regent's Park to the N.E. end of Ballards Lane, Finchley. Quite a large part of its route lay in Hendon and the road enters the parish near to The Castle at Childs Hill. This road, like the Edgware Road, was a turnpike road and toll gates were erected to collect the dues from passengers. A report of the Commissioners of the Metropolitan Turnpike Roads Trust drawn up in 1827 mentions that although much improvement has been made, the materials used locally were scarce and of poor quality. Since the road ran over heavy clay, it needed care and attention, particularly to the drainage. It was recommended that efforts should be made to open (gravel) pits in the locality so that materials could be obtained during the summer. The Vestry appointed Surveyors who were responsible for the maintenance of the roads – by 1791, 10 of these were necessary although, of course, these were still unpaid. It was not until 1837 that a paid surveyor was appointed at a salary of £50 per year. Some differences of opinion existed between the Vestry and the Lord of the Manor as to the responsibility for the bridges and in 1758 the parish brought an indictment against the Lord of the Manor for failing to repair the Silk Stream bridge on the Edgware Road.

Some typical entries in the Surveyor's Accounts for 1827 are as follows:

	£	s.	d.
Mr. Brooke for 107 loads of gravel @ 1/3	6	13	9
The Commissioners of the Metropolitan Roads			
1 year's Composition to Michaelmas 1827	23	5	0
Mr. Hill for 2 wheelbarrows	2	2	0
Mr. Alexander for 45 days of gravel carting	27	0	0
Postage for letters and stamps		19	0
For beer for gravel carters and diggers	2	8	3
For 20 loads of picked stones	3	0	0
Labourers working on the road were paid			
Jas. Lore 89 days @ 2/–	8	18	0
Jas. Abbey 174 days @ 1/10	14	10	0

The total expenditure for the year came to £220.2.11.

Williams v Wilberforce

Although the old family names continue to occur in the Church-wardens' Accounts, Vestry Minutes and the Accounts of the Overseers of the Poor and the Surveyors of the Highways, the newer residents were not slow in taking their part in local administration. This participation occasionally led to clashes with the 'establishment', two examples of these clashes concerned that formidable figure the Rev Theodore Williams, Vicar of Hendon from 1812 to 1875 and who died in harness at the age of 90. The first was a dispute between Williams and William Wilberforce who lived at Highwood Hill, Mill Hill during the last years of his life. Wilberforce had sought a faculty to build a chapel in his own grounds for the use of his family. However by the time that Williams got to hear of the plan the project seems to have grown to envisage a church at Mill Hill with its own incumbent. Previously, all the churchgoers in the whole parish of Hendon had had to make their way to St Mary's Hendon, a

D

journey of some distance from Mill Hill, so that some families maintained coach houses at Church End to house their carriages during service time. To them, a church at Mill Hill would be a boon, but Williams perhaps foresaw the loss of revenue from his wealthier pew renters. He opposed the plan bitterly in a series of letters to the Bishop of London and felt sufficiently strongly to have these letters and the affidavits he had secured from builders testifying to the shoddy materials used in the building, published at his own expense. However the church, now St Paul's, Mill Hill, was built and still stands in defiance of the affidavits. It was consecrated in 1833, shortly after Wilberforce's death.

Another incident involving a clash between Williams and his vestry occurred at a Vestry meeting at which Williams would have been ex-officio chairman and which had been convened for the purpose of declaring a rate. Williams was late for the meeting and in his absence one of the vestrymen had taken the chair and a rate had been made. Contrary to past custom Williams' own Vicarage had been made liable to rate. After the Vicar's belated arrival he forced the withdrawal of the acting chairman and proceeded to undo all that had been agreed. This led to hard words and a near-brawl. As the meeting was taking place in the usual room in the Greyhound Inn, a room which had been built over the churchyard, Williams summoned the offending vestrymen for brawling on consecrated ground and caused them to be fined heavily.

Wilberforce was an excellent example of the kind of person who came to live in Hendon but who had their living elsewhere. Others included his friend Sir Stamford Raffles, Peter Collinson, Charles Johnson, Mark Lemon, Nathaniel Hone, Abraham Raimbach, Sir William Anderson and Sir Charles Flower.

The growth of population

Perhaps the best indication of the accelerated rate of change can be seen by a study of the population figures. In 1700 the population was about 1,900, by 1801 this had only increased to 1,955, a growth of only 55 in 100 years! But by 1811, only ten years later the population had grown to 2,589, an increase of 594 in ten years. The number of houses in 1821, 450, shows an increase of fifty over that in 1811, 399. Of the population in 1811, about 60 were in receipt of relief from the poor rate while a further twenty three were housed in the workhouse.

The Parish of Hendon had set up a workhouse at the end of the Burroughs in about 1735 and this establishment had continued for about 100 years until by the Act of 1834 parishes were allowed to combine into Unions for the purpose of poor relief and finally the Hendon Union workhouse was set up in 1862 in the Edgware Road. This was shared with the parishes of Edgware, Great and Little Stanmore, Harrow, Kingsbury, Pinner, Willesden and Twyford Abbey.

Perhaps the best picture of Hendon as it was in the early years of the nineteenth century can be obtained from the following extracts from Lewis' Topographical Dictionary of England.

Hendon (St Mary), a parish, and the head of a union, in the hundred of Gore, county of Middlesex ... 3150 inhabitants ... The village is pleasantly situated on an eminence, in a small vale watered by the river Brent, over which is an ancient bridge of stone; the houses are irregularly built; in the neighbourhood are many handsome villas, and the environs abound with rural walks and agreeable scenery ... A court leet for the manor is held on the Tuesday before Whitsuntide, and a court baron occasionally [At the White Bear] ... The church is a spacious structure in the decorated English style with some small Norman remains and a square embattled tower ... A church was erected on Mill Hill in the later English style, at the expense of the late William Wilberforce, Esq. There are places of worship for Independents and Wesleyans. A school-room for boys was erected ... and a National school is supported by subscription. Robert Daniels Esq. of London in 1681 bequeathed £2000 for the erection and endowment of an almshouse for ten aged men and women ... Six almshouses were erected in 1696 by Thomas Nichol who endowed them for aged persons. At Mill Hill is the Protestant Dissenters' grammar-school, founded in 1807, and erected on the site of the residence of Peter Collinson, Esq., an eminent naturalist at an expense of £25,000.

This was written in 1842 and the same book contains a description of Edgware, parts of which are as follows:

EDGWARE (St Margarets) a parish (formerly a market town) in the union of Hendon, hundred of Gore, county of Middlesex . . . containing 645 inhabitants. This place from its situation within a pleasant distance of the metropolis, and the excellence of the road leading to it through an almost uninterrupted succession of elegant villas and agreeable scenery, has become the residence of numerous opulent and respectable families. The Norman Watling Street, leading to the ancient city of Verulam, passes over a bridge near the entrance to the village, which consists of one principal street, of which the western side is in the parish of Little Stanmore, or Whitchurch, where in the early part of the eighteenth century, James, Duke of Chandos, at an expense of £250,000, erected the magnificent palace of Canons . . . The village contains several respectable houses, and is supplied with water from a well, dug in 1822, by public subscription. The market, formerly on Thursday, has been discontinued but a fair is still held on the first Wednesday, Thursday and Friday in August for cattle and toys: on the two last days races are held which are in general well attended . . . There are courts baron and leet on the first of May . . . The parish comprises of 1,968 acres of which 165 are arable, 1,758 meadow and pasture and about 45 woodland . . . The church, with the exception of its square embattled tower, which is of flint and stone, was rebuilt of brick in 1763, and the interior thoroughly repaired in 1822. An almshouse for four aged women was founded in 1680 by Samuel Atkinson . . . Charles Day Esq. in 1828 founded almshouses for eight aged persons.

Yet another contemporary description in 1819 draws this picture of Hendon.

The beauty of its situation and the easy distance from London, have induced many to select this place for their country residence . . . Mill

Hill is a fine swell of ground, rising to a considerable elevation, and commanding a wide extent of prospect, in which Windsor Castle may be observed. The houses in this situation form a considerable village in which are some respectable family residences . . . At the lower part of the [Brent] Street, a bridge over the Brent leads to Golders Green which is pleasantly situated, and contains many ornamental villas and plantations . . .

The coming of the railway

From these descriptions of rural serenity it can be seen that the Industrial Revolution had had little effect on Hendon. Agriculture was the principal industry and this supported in turn a number of crafts such as blacksmithing and farriery. Other industries of which we have a note at this time were some brick kilns situated in Childs Hill and the emergence of a hand-laundry industry in the same area. This serenity continued undisturbed until the middle of the nineteenth century until, in fact, the coming of the railway in 1867 to both Hendon and Edgware.

The Great Northern, Edgware line was opened from Finsbury Park on 22 August 1867. From Church End, Finchley to Edgware the line was single throughout and was worked on the staff system. There were very few signals, one being a tall platform signal at Edgware station and another being near the Deans Lane Bridge. Leaving Finchley the line descended steeply for about a mile, crossing the thirteen-arch viaduct over Dollis Brook to reach Mill Hill East. It passed under the Midland Railway line and terminated in the country station of what was then the old-world village of Edgware. The line fell into disuse after the opening of the High Barnet branch in 1872 and continued as a shuttle service for just a few trains a day. It is now no longer used and a block of offices now stands on the site of the station, although London Transport trains run to Mill Hill East. The Midland Railway's London extension was opened for goods and coal traffic to Brent and St Pancras in early September 1867. The station buildings and approaches at Hendon and Mill Hill were nearing completion in December 1867 but on the night of the 14th the station buildings at Hendon caught fire and considerable damage was done. Energetic efforts were made to restore the buildings and by March 1868 Hendon and Mill Hill were ready to receive local goods traffic. Passenger services were begun in October 1868 with some nine trains a day to Moorgate Street.

This opening of communications direct to the heart of London's business centre had an immediate and direct effect on Hendon. Although unfortunately the station at Hendon was some distance from the village centre near the Church there was an immense growth of house building. Some of this at the Cricklewood end of the Parish was to serve as housing for railway workers on the sidings nearby, while the area near the station was soon covered by houses built by speculative builders for city clerks and merchants. Again, the best guide to these changes can be seen from the population figures.

During the years 1831–51 the population increased by about 200 to 3,333 but between 1851 and 1871 it more than doubled to 6,972.

Victorian holidays in Hendon

It was not only housing and industry that the railway encouraged. The Welsh Harp – the body of water formed by the damming of the Brent just below its junction with Silkstream and which was used to maintain the level of the Grand Union Canal – was already the site of two inns and because of the fishing and sporting facilities offered by the water and because of the closeness of the Kingsbury racecourse, a rendezvous at holiday times. But in May 1870 the Midland Railway, urged by the landlord of the Welsh Harp inn (already a popular centre of entertainment), opened a station nearby and for about the next thirty years the people of London flocked there in their thousands to enjoy all the fun of the fair and a wide range of sporting activities. A newspaper report of 1891 describes the scene as follows:

Immediately opposite the Welsh Harp stands a large piece of ground covered with temporary erections. Coconut-shies, Aunt Sallies and rifle galleries – all were doing a roaring trade . . . A comparative novelty at Hendon in the way of amusement is the aerial switchback. On payment of a penny you are provided with a sort of wheel with a handle to it; you place the wheel on a wire stretched between two supports, one higher than the other, and if you grasp the handle firmly enough you are whirled from one end of the wire to the other . . . Many of the appliances were very elaborate. The wooden horses not only went round, but they switched gracefully up and down; and besides horses to ride on they had elephants and tigers as well.

In 1891 also at the Welsh Harp a French aeronaut was advertised as making an ascent of 5,000 feet in his 'Patent Parachute Balloon'. There was confusion at the moment of launching and the whole apparatus sank to the ground. Cheated of their spectacle the rougher elements in the crowd demanded their money back and M. Capazza required police escort to get him back to the shelter of the Inn.

Victorian Hendon

In the 1860s Hendon was a great haymaking district and Irish farm labourers came over in great numbers bringing their own scythes to cut the grass and to make the hay. They brought little else besides their scythes and their luggage was no more than could be carried in a large handkerchief. If the summer was wet and cold these Irish labourers and their families suffered terribly since they had only open barns and sheds to sleep in. The local people fed them as best they could. At this time much of the area was still open country and there was little or no local transport. A horse bus came out from London Bridge as far as Jack Straw's Castle at Hampstead and a little later a local service of sorts existed between the Bell and the

Station. Education in Hendon was carried on in the National Schools at Church End (now St Mary's C. of E.) and the central portion of the present primary school was built in 1857 at the expense of the second Lord Tenterden. At Mill Hill the Charity School continued as a National School (now St Paul's C. of E.). Another National School replaced the old Dame school at Childs Hill in 1856 (this is now All Saints C. of E.) and yet another opened at St Peter's, Cricklewood in 1882. A British Day School was started at Childs Hill in 1870 and this continued until it was taken over by the newly formed School Board in 1897 for in Hendon no compulsory school rate was levied until that date, although a voluntary rate had existed since 1870. By the following year the Board had responsibility for the British Schools at New Brent Street and at Childs Hill and a Free Church School at West Hendon. At the same time six Church of England schools and three Roman Catholic schools existed. The Board opened its own first school in 1901 at Burnt Oak and others followed in Bell Lane, Algernon Road and Childs Hill later in that year. In 1872 the shape of local government underwent a further change. The vestry which had managed local affairs for so long was displaced by the Rural Sanitary Authority and for about five years Hendon fell within the area of the Edgware Rural Sanitary Authority. In 1877 the Hendon R.S.A. issued its own bye-laws but developments were so fast that by 1879 Hendon was constituted an Urban Sanitary Authority with 12 members representing 3 wards. In 1895 Hendon became an Urban District Council with 15 members representing 3 wards. In 1881 the first part-time Medical Officer of Health was appointed. The main preoccupation of the local authority was to develop the sewage system and by 1887 the drainage works was opened that dealt with the sewage of Hendon, although Mill Hill and the Hyde areas were still without. It was not almost until the end of the century that the greater part of the houses in the District were connected to main drains. An Infectious Diseases hospital was opened in 1890 and the

Central London Sick Asylum (now Colindale Hospital) was opened in 1898. The following year the council decided to provide an ambulance for infectious diseases. This accommodated two patients and one nurse and cost between 70 and 80 guineas. A Fire Brigade had existed since 1855 and two years later the Brigade purchased a Merrryweather manual fire engine. This was housed in what had been a coach house opposite the Greyhound Inn. In 1866 a Volunteer Fire Brigade was formed and by 1899, when the U.D.C. took control of fire protection, substations existed at Mill Hill and Childs Hill.

In 1866 Hendon was included in the limits of water supply of the West Middlesex Waterworks Company but even in 1873 many of the inhabitants drew their supply from pumps and wells. The Town pump was in Brent Street and there was another in the Hyde at the Hyde Brewery. The inhabitants of Edgware drew theirs from a well near the Parish Church. Water sellers did a good trade with water at 1d or 2d a pail. In that year the Colne Valley Water Co. obtained Parliamentary power to supply water in part of Hendon and in 1902 the West Middlesex Waterworks Company transferred their powers to the Metropolitan Water Board. In 1870 an omnibus ran daily from Hendon to the G.P.O. in London and another plied regularly between Hendon and Oxford Street via Cricklewood. A coach service existed between Mill Hill and London and carters' teams provided a service for parcels. Until 1871 the only street lighting was supplied by oil lamps but in that year gas lighting was introduced at Hendon and Childs Hill. In 1899 a Company was formed to obtain an Electric Lighting Order and this order was transferred to the Council in the same year. The coming of the electric lighting received strong local opposition from people who feared increases in the rates but the progressives won the day.

In those days at the end of the nineteenth century when there were no machine-made entertainments, no television, no cinema, the people of Hendon made their own entertainments. At the

Institution in Brent Street were the assembly rooms where the balls, concerts, bazaars and public meetings were held. The Hendon subscription dances were attended by all the local gentry and the musically minded could have joined the Hendon Choral Society. For the argumentative the Hendon Debating Society came into existence in 1879 and lasted for some 40 years. A quotation from a former Borough Librarian, J. E. Walker, in his 'Hendon 1851–1951' gives some idea of the activities.

There was also a Ratepayers' Association, Horticultural Society, Nursing Society, Co-operative Industrial Society, Total Abstinence Society and Band of Hope, Total Abstinence Sick Benefit Society, Sons of Temperance Benefit Society, the Rose and Crown Provident Society, Foresters, Oddfellows and the Oddfellows Brass Band. Yes, and there were two lending libraries, one as part of the activities of the Co-operative Society, the other in Fuller Street with Mrs Day as Hon. Secretary. It must have been a lively little community when it is remembered that the population at the 1881 census was only 10,484.

Behind the Institution where Brampton Grove is now, was the cricket field. The ledger of Hendon Cricket Club shows that it had a continuous life of forty years, from 1852 to 1892.

An amateur swimming club was also in existence but carried on their activities at the Finchley Road Baths.

THE TWENTIETH CENTURY

In 1900 the U.D.C's activities had so expanded that the staff were hard put to it to carry out their duties efficiently in what had been the Workhouse at the end of the Burroughs (now Quadrant Close). A foundation stone for the new Council Offices was laid, the offices themselves being opened with all due ceremony the following year. This building still forms the central portion of the Town Hall in the Burroughs. The Council administered the civic affairs of a population of 22,450, the rateable value of the district reaching the total of £154,398. For a time it would have appeared that any further growth would be slow. However, in 1902 work was begun on the extension of the Tube from Hampstead to Golders Green. Local property developers were quick to see the opportunities offered and by 1905 the first of the new houses at Golders Green were being built. In 1906 the Hampstead Garden Suburb Act was passed and the vision of Dame Henrietta Barnett began to take physical shape.

The coming of the Tube and the Garden Suburb

The tube extension was formally opened by the Rt Hon David Lloyd George, then President of the Board of Trade, in June 1907 and, for one day only, the public was invited to travel free of charge on what was described as 'the last link of a new chain of communication'. In fact, powers had already been secured for the extension later to Hendon and Edgware but no mention of this was made in the official publicity. It was at first intended to have an intermediate station between Hampstead and Golders Green. This was originally to be called North End but although the name was changed later to 'Bull and Bush' in fact the station never materialized and only exists in 'ghost' form, the platform levels being in place but no access shafts. By 1908 some 80 houses had been erected in the Garden Suburb and new roads were springing into existence in Golders Green (Golders Gardens, Gainsborough Gardens and Powis Gardens were cut in 1909). The Garden Suburb received the honour of a royal visit in 1910 when King George V and Queen Mary came to inspect this now flourishing venture. By 1911 the population had increased to 38,806 and this increase of nearly 17,000 in 10 years can be almost entirely ascribed to the effect of the opening of the Tube extension.

Hendon Aerodrome and Grahame-White

During the first decade of the twentieth century the thoughts of Hendonians were not only 'Underground' but 'in the air'. Local enthusiasts had been experimenting with flying machines during 1909 but in 1910 the *Daily Mail* offered a prize of £10,000 for an aeroplane flight from London to Manchester. The newspaper stipulated that the flight must pass within five miles of their offices. On April 21st 1910 Mr Claude Grahame-White made his first attempt to win the prize. He took off from Wormwood Scrubs and flew for some 83 miles to a spot near Rugby. After an hour's rest he took off again but after covering a total of 117 miles high winds and engine trouble brought him down near Lichfield. Unfortunately his machine was damaged by the high wind whilst on the ground and he was unable to continue. Meanwhile, the French aviator Paulhan had arrived in England with the intention of making an attempt on the prize. On April 27 Paulhan took off from Hendon and flew direct to Lichfield as the first stage. When Grahame-White heard that his rival had taken off, he himself started out from Wormwood Scrubs about an hour later but as darkness was falling he was forced to come down only about 60 miles from his starting point. Since he knew that his machine was slower and since Paulhan was already far ahead of him, Grahame-White decided after only a few hours rest to fly on through the night guided by the headlamps of cars or by the lights of the railway. He flew on until dawn but strong winds forced him down only 10 miles from the spot where Paulhan had spent the night. Paulhan took off at dawn and completed his flight to Manchester to win the prize. Grahame-White, though unsuccessful, became a popular hero and he flew with distinction at flying meetings around the country and in America. Returning to England at the end of the year in December 1910 he acquired the tract of land at Hendon from where his rival had taken off. As Managing Director of the Grahame-White Company he proceeded to convert the meadows into the London Aerodrome which was to become one of the best known and completely organized flying grounds in the world. In 1911 Grahame-White invited public support for a company called Grahame-White, Bleriot, Maxim Ltd., but since only about one third of the capital was subscribed, he returned this money and formed the Grahame-White Aviation Company not without prophesies of doom from his friends. His confidence was justified and in the first year alone the gate receipts totalled £11,000 and this sum increased year by year. Grahame-White was a great propagandist for air power and worked hard to interest the Government in its potentialities. In 1911 the First U.K. Aerial Post was flown from Hendon to Windsor and some 130,000 letters and cards were carried by the Company's pilots. Hendon Aerodrome, with its flying displays and aerial races, became an event in the social calendar, rivalling Ascot and Epsom. Exhibitions of night flying and naval and military displays were also held. At the same time the Grahame-White company was engaged in building aircraft and with the coming of the 1914 war it went into full production. So great was the effort required that Grahame-White was allowed to relinquish his commission in the Royal Naval Air Service to concentrate on the work of training pilots and building planes. Some idea of the growth of the Company can be gained from the fact that it employed only 20 before the outbreak of hostilities and that by the end of the war it employed 3,000. The people of Hendon flocked to the Aerodrome to watch the displays though many of them took up their viewpoint on the slopes of Sunnyhill where the flying could be watched free of charge.

Industry and Transport

In 1894 the Metropolitan Tramways & Omnibus Company Ltd had been formed with the intention of building and operating tramways in the northern and north-western outskirts of London. In 1901, after a change of name to the Metropolitan Electric Tramways Ltd, the decision was made to start by electrifying those routes at that time operated by horse trams, and agreements were entered into with the County Council to build new routes. This work began in 1902, but it was not until 1904 that a route within what are now Hendon's borough boundaries became operative. This was the route connecting 'The Crown' at Cricklewood to Edgware (Church Lane).

By 1907 a route was working between Edgware and Canons Park, and in 1909 routes between North Finchley and Golders Green and between Golders Green and the Hampstead boundary were added. In the same year the link between Cricklewood and Childs Hill ('The Castle') was opened.

The 1920s were probably the heyday of the electric tram, for in 1936 the whole western system was converted to trolleybus operation. This decision affected the Hendon Depot, which also included a works manufacturing and overhauling trams.

It is interesting to note that an early experimental trolleybus was tried out within the Hendon Depot in 1909. This was a single-deck chain-driven vehicle, fitted with solid tyres. This experimental trolleybus was numbered 1 and carried route boards indicating a service from Hendon to Golders Green via The Burroughs, Brent Street and Golders Green Road. Nothing came of this experiment, however.

Before the coming of the steam railways Hendon's only connections with London by public transport were originally by coach and later by omnibus. A hundred years ago the horse-bus left each day on its journey from the 'Angel and Crown' at Mill Hill, through Brent Street and Hampstead to Tottenham Court Road and on to the Bank. On the return journey the bus left the Bank at 4.45 p.m. and the fare was 2s 0d from Mill Hill and 1s 6d from Hendon, with a reduction of sixpence if the passenger was seated outside.

Edward Sutton, who ran this horse-bus service, suffered a setback when the Midland Railway was opened, and attempted to offset his losses by running a feeder service to the station at Hendon, which was situated some distance from the village. In 1868 a horse-bus service ran from Hendon to the newly opened Swiss Cottage Station, and this was run by a Mr E. Woodland, who ceased operating in 1878. Joseph Camp soon afterwards instituted a short-lived service five times a day from the 'White Bear' in the Burroughs. Another service in the 1870s ran from Brent Street and along the Edgware Road to the Marble Arch four times a day. By the 1880s Golders Green residents had a service of twenty minutes' interval only running through Finchley to Oxford Circus.

With the turn of the century came the motor-bus, and by 1912 at least two routes were operating: the 83 from Golders Green to Station Road, Hendon, and the 13 from 'The Bell' to London Bridge. In the same year the London General Omnibus Company demolished Ravensfield Manor in the Burroughs and erected their bus garage on the site. By 1923 a further route connecting Golders Green to Harrow via Mill Hill had been inaugurated, and by 1928 the official 'Guide to Hendon' merely records that 'The motor omnibus services are numerous and most convenient and connect with the City and West End.'

In 1921 Handley Page Ltd, the first company to be constituted exclusively for the design and manufacture of aeroplanes, moved into the district. In its heyday both Handley Page's aerodrome at Cricklewood and Grahame-White's at Hendon were flourishing whilst yet another aerodrome – de Havilland's was operating just beyond the boundaries of the borough at Stag Lane.

At least two local newspapers served the district, the *Hendon & Finchley Times* since 1875 and the *Golders Green Gazette* since 1880. In 1913 the *Hendon & Finchley Times* recorded the opening of the Cottage Hospital and also of the Hendon Court House. Anna Pavlova came to live at Ivy House in Golders Green and in the following year the theatre, where in December 1930 she was to make the last appearance before the public, the Golders Green Hippodrome, was opened. In the year 1914 at first unshadowed by the War to come, Hendon's mind was focused on civic matters. A new central Fire Station was opened in the Burroughs and plans were being discussed for a building combining a swimming bath and a public library, to take its place between the Council Offices and the new fire station.

The Great War

This was not to be, however, for in the number of the *Hendon & Finchley Times* dated August 7, 1914 the formal declaration of War between England and Germany issued to the Foreign Office was reprinted. Beneath this the following appeal was printed.

TO OUR READERS
KEEP COOL

All our readers have the opportunity of sharing their patriotism at this time of national danger. If they cannot all go to the war they can at least prevent panic at home, and especially can the women folk do this. We appeal to them not to lay in abnormal stores of foodstuffs and thus create a shortage that will run up prices, and be the means of depriving poorer folk of bare necessities. There is an ample supply of foodstuffs in the country or coming through; prices doubtless will range a little higher on account of the increased difficulty of transit, and some luxuries will become scarce, but there is absolutely no need for the un-English behaviour of those people who have been laying in stores even beyond that which they can possibly use whilst consumable.

Reports of local inhabitants being called to the colours appeared in the same number and bus services were temporarily suspended, 40 men from the bus garage being called up. Horses were in as much demand as men and Messrs Schweppes who had been established on the Edgware Road since the early 1890s placed 50 at the disposal of the Government. The following week saw the departure of the 5th Battalion of the Middlesex Regiment from Mill Hill. Some 1,000 pints of cocoa were served to the departing heroes by the ladies of Mill Hill. The following day the Hendon Battalion of the National Reserves paraded at the Drill Hall in Algernon Road, and a recruiting sermon was preached from the pulpit of the Parish Church. About two weeks later a roll call of the men of Hendon who were serving King and Country was published in the *Hendon & Finchley Times* (2,500 by December 1914), while the citizens left at home formed Relief Committees to enquire into cases of distress arising through the War. The ladies of the churches formed a Mending Committee and the local laundries offered to wash for the troops. An invasion of Hendon by 'Germans' was reported in the *Hendon & Finchley Times* – September 1914, but the 'enemy' were in fact actors in a film being made in the grounds of Burroughs Lodge depicting a sham battle between Belgians and Germans. The same number of the Times listed the amounts payable to households where troops were billeted. Lodging, Breakfast, Dinner and Supper for one man totalled 3s 4½d, whilst stabling and food for one horse totalled 2s 7½d.

After the first excitement of the war had died down life began to return to some sort of normality and by October 9, 1914 the

Hendon & Finchley Times editorial was concerned with the increase in rateable value of the district.

Although regrettably the list of Hendon men who had lost their lives in the War grew each week and although few families passed through the War without the loss of some loved one, the War actually made little physical effect on Hendon. In fact as an advertisement inserted by a Finchley grocer in the Christmas number 1914 stated 'The Englishman's motto – Business as usual'.

It was decided to defer the building of a swimming bath in the Burroughs for a time and in fact the project never materialized. The year 1913 had seen the last entry in the Vestry Minute books and in 1916 the last Court of the Manor of Hendon was held in the traditional meeting place at the White Bear. The abolition of copyhold tenure in 1922 would see the end of the Manor Courts, although in fact the last entry in the Court Books was dated August 8, 1934. The aeronautical firms received a great boost from the demand for military aircraft and in 1917 Handley Page took over the aerodrome near their works at Cricklewood. By the following year some important first flights had been made from this aerodrome. These included the first flight to India in (a) a two-engined machine and (b) in a four-engined machine.

The Armistice in 1918 was greeted with local celebrations. When the maroons signalled the Armistice there was a few moments' pause, for previously they had been ominous sounds. As soon as their import was realized the picture changed. Flags appeared everywhere, school children were dismissed for the day, many factories closed and shops did little business. So many people wanted to get to Town to join in the celebrations there that police had to be called to control the crowds at the bus stopping point at the Bell. Later in the evening more serious minded citizens crowded the churches at special services held at 7 p.m.

The War made vast changes in the social life of the people of

Hendon. Some indication of the rises in wages and prices can be obtained from these figures.

In 1914 an assistant council schoolmaster was paid on a scale of £110–275 per annum and an assistant schoolmistress on a scale of £95–180. In 1918 new scales were introduced by the Hendon Education Committee who stated with justifiable pride that the new scales were probably among the best in the country. The schoolmaster was to be paid on a scale of £120–325 and his female colleague on a scale of £110–250. Miss E. C. Growse, the only lady representative on the committee, after making strenuous but unsuccessful efforts for equal pay, joined in the approval of the new scales. Advertisements for cook generals in 1914 offered wages of £18–20 per year, by 1918 £30 per year seems to have been an average wage.

Post War Flying at Hendon

After the War the Aerodrome reverted to its peacetime uses and in an article in the *Hendon & Finchley Times*, Mr Warden mused on the past, present and future of the aerodrome in these terms.

I looked along Sunny Hill Fields and thought of my boyhood days. How many generations of London lovers have walked over these famous fields. In the distance I saw the St Joseph Catholic Training Missionary College, and there in the clear sky stood the spire of Harrow Old Church. Farther off lies Windsor Castle on its hill, visible on a bright summer day with no haze.

Dipping down into the hollow were those graceful slopes where as children we tobogganed. Old fashioned winters seem to be the rule then . . . the toboggan was the *ne plus ultra* of travel. There were no aeroplanes.

There still are the shining lines of the railway. When we were boys it was one of the delights of a summer evening to go out to watch the Scotch Express pass. The mile and a half of stretch of embankment between Mill Hill and Colindale was covered 'by the snorting monster' in less than two minutes. We used to think it marvellous. And so it was . . . When I first knew Hendon, aeroplanes were not known . . . It was a pretty village, a little too far from London to attract visitors. On Bank Holiday, it is true, Mr Warner and his famous Welsh Harp brought down a swarm of pleasure makers of a sort . . . In this pretty little world, away from the bustle and roar of London, we were tranquil and refreshed by the sight and sounds of nature . . . Corn grew high in the fields which one traversed by a barely marked sheep track. Cattle grazed placidly on the pasture from Hinge's fields to as far as the eye could reach; and rich meadows were to be seen on every hand.

Much later on when the first beginnings of aviation moved the popular imagination, it was to Hendon that the airmen came. Saturday after Saturday in those early years before the war there were little crowds of visitors to the first primitive ground used for flying. Then motor buses were put on the route. The village had already become a suburb; now it became a town. Along the high road ran the tram, and the number of tea-shops which were opened up began to give the place an air of importance.

Flying was still something wonderful and those Saturday afternoons around the aerodrome will be long remembered . . . The pioneers . . . thrilled the spectators simply by rising in the air and when the loop was first looped over Hendon it was regarded as the most daring performance that had ever been seen . . . Seated in little groups one took tea and watched the evolutions. It was an agreeable way of passing an idle hour in which there was sure to be some exciting incident. For aeroplanes used to fall at that time fairly frequently. They could not be relied upon to remain in the air and nasty landings were common.

Such was Hendon of the past as I remember it. What of Hendon to-day. Today, Hendon is a busy centre of aviation. There were . . . the Grahame White Aerodrome, those of the Airco Company at Kingsbury and a little higher up the Edgware Road at Cricklewood were those of the Handley Page Company. What I saw now was that immense tract of fields surrounded by an incredible number of hangar sheds and workshops. A curious contrast of big and little machines all lying together like eagles and sparrows in the same nest; workmen's houses clustering thickly; factories where they make all sorts of aeroplane accessories. This was the new Hendon. The air, if not thick with aeroplanes, at all events studded with them. White wings flashing and turning in the sunlight. There was a continuous hum in the air as the machines came and went on their aerial mission.

The writer went on to describe a Hendon of the future, as a Clapham Junction or a Crewe of the Universe. Unfortunately this was not to be. A dispute arose between Grahame-White and the Air Ministry as to ownership of the aerodrome. Just before the end of the War the Grahame-White Co. had been given orders for hundreds of aircraft. These orders were now cancelled by the Air Ministry and Grahame-White found himself in considerable difficulties. He attempted to use the production potentiality of his factory by manufacturing motorcars and furniture. But in 1922 his hopes were dashed when the Treasury took possession of his factory and all his Hendon property and discharged his staff and employees. A long legal battle ensued which resulted in the Air Ministry assuming control of the aerodrome after payment of a considerable sum to Grahame-White. Hendon Aerodrome became an R.A.F. station, the scene of the thrilling Air Displays that delighted thousands in the years between the wars. But the vision of Hendon as a centre of civil air communication proved an illusion. The increasing size of aircraft and the increasing rate of house building made Hendon unsuitable for intensive air activity. It had a short revival of life during the Second World War although it only briefly served as a first line fighter station. Within 10 years of the ending of the War, flying had virtually ceased, although the Air Ministry retained control, using the facilities there as a staging point for military personnel and their families.

The Extension of the Underground and Further Population Growth

In 1912 the population of Hendon reached 57,529, an increase of nearly 20,000 in 10 years. Shortly afterwards work was begun on the extension of the Underground through to Edgware. Hendon Central was opened for traffic in November 1923 and the line through to Edgware in August 1924. Because of a builders' strike it was not possible to complete Burnt Oak station in time for the opening and it was brought into use in October 1924. In the five year plan projected by L.P.T.B. in 1935 an extension from Edgware to Aldenham with intermediate stations at Brockley Hill and Elstree was envisaged. This extension has in fact never materialized although some work on the route was carried out.

In 1924 the L.C.C. obtained possession of the Goldbeater Farm Estates for a town planning project which was to be called the Watling Estate. Work began in 1926 and the first houses occupied in 1927. Within 12 months 2,100 families moved in and by 1930 the whole estate of over 4,000 dwellings was completed. The population of the estate at that time was about 20,000. The influx of working class families brought some protests from the residents of nearby Mill Hill with its predominantly middle-class population. In 1927 a Watling Residents' Association was formed which was to flourish and build its own community centre and to work hard for the needs of the residents.

The New Roads – the Disappearance of Rural Hendon

At the same time as the extension of the Underground, work was being taken in hand for the construction of new main roads. The Hendon Way began construction from Finchley Road in 1924 and the Barnet Way was started at the same time. In the following year the Hendon section of the North Circular Road was built and the Great North Way was built in 1926. By that year the Hendon Way was completed from Finchley Road to the North Circular. Its continuation to the N.W. border of Hendon was far enough advanced for that section to be opened in 1927. New roads called for new and reconstructed bridges. Finchley Lane Bridge was built in 1926, Bunns Bridge in 1927, Stoneyfield Bridge in 1928, while the Mutton Bridge in Bell Lane was rebuilt in 1931. By that year there were more than 110 miles of public highway in the district. As these new roads opened up the district for housing, so the farms that had once been the mainstay of life began to disappear. The melancholy roll-call of the dates of demolition is as follows:

Goldbeaters Farm	1924
Dollis Farm	1930
Cowhouse Farm	1931
Uphill Farm	1931
Mill Hill Farm	1933
Decoy Farm	1935
Dole Street Farm	1937

The new roads and new railways so encouraged new housing that by 1931 the population had soared to 115,682 and by 1939 the estimated population was 169,765. At that time the Borough Council alone had built nearly 1,300 dwellings. Although the Urban District Council had adopted the Libraries Act in 1919, work on building a Central Library did not begin until 1929. The building was opened in December of that year but school libraries organized by the Council had been in operation since 1927. A programme of branch libraries was called for and before the War brought an end to building, libraries had been opened at Golders Green, 1935 and Mill Hill, 1937.

The Incorporation of the Borough of Hendon

In 1931 Edgware Parish became part of the Hendon Urban District and the Council was composed of 33 members representing 9 wards. This, however, was just a preliminary to the incorporation as a Borough by a Charter granted in 1932. The Council then was composed of 9 aldermen and 27 councillors representing 9 wards. The area of the new borough was 10,471 acres and it was about 7·3 miles long and 3·6 miles wide. The rateable value was £1,424,720. The Borough Council developed the resources of the area quickly. In 1935 the Mill Hill swimming pool was added to that built in West Hendon in 1922. The Town Hall was extended in 1934 and a Health Centre was built in the same year. A further Health Centre next to the library at Mill Hill was opened in 1937. Planning schemes were instituted in 1936 and 1939 although the War brought them both to a standstill.

The years just before the outbreak of the War saw the development of that cosmopolitan characteristic which makes Hendon unique among London suburbs. As early as 1922 a Synagogue was consecrated in Dunstan Road, Golders Green. The building was actually completed in 1927 and in the same year another synagogue was begun just off Brent Street. This moved into its permanent home in an imposing building in Raleigh Close which was completed in 1935. (Another Synagogue was eventually built on the Brent Street Site.) From 1933 to 1939 many refugees from Nazi Germany found shelter in Hendon so that in an estimate made in 1959 it was stated that more than a quarter of the population of Hendon were Jewish. There has always been the happiest of co-operation between Jew and Christian in Hendon.

Hendon and its people played a full part in the second World War. Although not suffering the full force of the blitz that fell upon Central London and many provincial centres, Hendon had more than its share of bombs. The aircraft and other industries strung along the Edgware Road, together with the nearby aerodrome and railway installations, made it an inviting target. By the end of the War nearly 600 H.E. bombs alone had been dropped on the Borough together with innumerable incendiaries. Nearly 250 people were killed and over 1,300 injured. Some 18,000 houses were damaged. The greater part of the damage was caused in 1940 and 1941 and the bitterest blow was the incident at West Hendon when one bomb laid waste three roads, killed over 70 people and made 1,500 homeless. The people of Hendon didn't take this punishment lying down. They served in A.R.P., the Fire Service, the W.V.S. and the Royal Observer Corps, they organized meals services and British Restaurants, they did what they could to provide comfort for the troops. They adopted the cruiser H.M.S. Ursa and developed a link between ship and borough. Most spectacular of all the campaigns, however, was undoubtedly the Four Fighter Fund which raised the money to buy four Spitfires. These were named Pegasus, Griffin, Endeavour and Lamb, the names being taken from elements in the Borough's coat of arms. Even during the darkest days of the war Hendonians occasionally relaxed and the first of the Hendon Shows was held in the Borough Playing Fields in 1943. In the year that the War ended Hendon was divided into two parliamentary constituencies, a move that had been foreshadowed by the Boundary commission that had sat the year before. Since the population was estimated to be nearly 150,000 it was a well-warranted division. Thus the Hendon Parliamentary Division which had existed since 1919 became Hendon North and Hendon South. The population continued to rise until 1948 when an estimated total of 160,000 was reached. Since that date the number has declined as building activities in the rural areas bordering on Hendon have relieved the pressure on housing in the Borough.

Post War Hendon to the present day

The years that followed the end of the War were austere years. Food rationing continued and there were periodic shortages in many basic commodities. The Borough Council pressed on with housing development as best they could and it is to their credit that in the seven years from 1945 they built nearly 1,300 dwellings. Most of these were normal house units but the emphasis for Council building in recent years has been on multi-storey flats. The first major achievement in this field was the development at Spur Road. These skyscraper flats were officially opened by H.M. The Queen Mother in 1959. The Council also took up their plans for the development of the library service but since building was restricted they inaugurated a Travelling Library Service in 1947. In 1950 they opened a temporary library in Truth Hall at Edgware and in the same year acquired a site for a permanent building. A prefabricated building was opened on this site in 1952 and this was replaced by the present modern building in 1961. In 1954 a branch was opened at Burnt Oak and in 1962 the latest addition, a branch at Childs Hill, was opened. Road widening and lighting improvements were carried out as soon as conditions allowed and plans are presently in hand for the extension of the motorway through Hendon and the construction of a flyover at Brent Cross. Many of these future developments were put on show to the ratepayers in an exhibition entitled 'Hendon of Tomorrow' which was mounted at the Church Farm House Museum in 1961. This building, a seventeenth-century farm house, had been acquired by the Borough Council in 1944 and had been used as temporary housing for a time. This use was discontinued after a while and the building remained empty for a year or two. Considerable discussion as to its future took place and it was not until 1956, after extensive reconstruction, that it was opened as a Museum of local history. At the last census in 1961 the population totalled 151,500 and the rateable value stood at £3,600,467. Of a total area of 10,371 acres, 1,478 acres have been preserved as open space by the Borough Council and a further 113 acres by the London County Council in Golders Hill Park and the Hampstead Heath extension. Now with the proposal by the Government that Hendon should be merged with the Borough of Finchley and with the U.D.C's of Barnet, East Barnet and Friern Barnet, Hendon stands once more at the threshold of a new era of development and the year 1963 seems an appropriate moment to bring this brief history to a close.

1086 – 200 – 250 (Males 45)
1700 – 1,900
1801 – 1,955
1811 – 2,589
1821 – 3,100
1831 – 3,100
1851 – 3,333
1871 – 6,972
1881 – 10,484
1891 – 15,843
1901 – 22,450
1911 – 38,806
1921 – 57,529
1931 – 115,529
1937 – 162,079
1939 – 169,765
1943 – 132,837
1944 – 135,344
1945 – 140,000
1946 – 151,000
1948 – 160,000
1949 – 157,000
1950 – 156,000
1951 – 155,690 (Ration Books 30.4.51)
   – 155,835 (Census 8.4.51)
1961 – 151,500

A SELECT BIBLIOGRAPHY

In addition to the card catalogues of the local history collection and the collection of the Mill Hill and Hendon Historical Society, both housed in the Reference Library at the Central Library, other bibliographies may be found in:

The Middlesex County Bibliography, Volume 2	1959
Middlesex and Hertfordshire Notes and Queries, Volume 1–4	1895–8

AGRICULTURE

P. Foot	General view of the agriculture of the County of Middlesex	1794
J. Middleton	View of the agriculture of Middlesex	1798
W. Page, *editor*	Victoria County History of Middlesex Volume 2	1911

ARCHAEOLOGY

J. A. Brown	Palaeolithic man in N.W. Middlesex	1887
North Middlesex Archaeological Research Committee	The Roman settlement on Brockley Hill: a brief account	[1952]
K. M. Richardson	Report on the excavations at Brockley Hill	1947
Sir Montague Sharpe	Antiquities of Middlesex: Middlesex in British, Roman and Saxon times	1919
P. G. Suggett	Sulloniacae: the Roman town on Brockley Hill	1952
C. E. Vulliamy	Archaeology of Middlesex and London	1930

AVIATION

F. Field and N. C. Baldwin	The Coronation aerial post, 1911	1934
Grahame-White Aviation Co. Ltd	The Birthplace of aerial power	1919
Hendon Public Libraries	Bibliography of aviation in Hendon	1957
Hendon Public Libraries	Chronology of flying in Hendon, 1862–1945	1955
J. Hopkins	Hendon and the art of flying	1955
G. G. O. Manton	Memories of the Old Masters	1936
R. Palmer	London's first airport	1954
C. Martin Sharp	D.H. an outline of De Havilland history	1960
G. Wallace	Flying witness	1955
G. Wallace	Claude Grahame-White	1960

BUILDINGS

N. G. Brett-James	The story of Hendon: manor and parish	1931
F. C. Eeles	The Parish Church of St Mary, Hendon	1931
E. T. Evans	The History and topography of the Parish of Hendon	1890
Hendon Borough Council	Church Farm House Museum	1955
N. Pevsner	The buildings of England: Middlesex	1951

A large number of sales catalogues describing various estates, houses and their contents are kept in the local history collection, and provide an invaluable aid in the study of older buildings in Hendon.

COMMUNICATIONS

E. F. Carter	Historical geography of the railways of the British Isles	1959
D. G. Denoon	Hendon highways	1936
C. H. Ellis	The Midland Railway	1953
G. F. A. Wilmor	The Railway in Finchley	1962

W. G. Passingham	The Romance of London's Underground	1932
M. Robbins	Middlesex	1953
E. G. Barnes	Notes on the history of railways in Hendon (Typewritten script)	1960

EDUCATION

N. G. Brett-James	The History of Mill Hill School, 1807–1923	[1923]
N. G. Brett-James	Mill Hill	1938
T. Constantinides	The Story of Hendon St Mary's Church of England Schools, 1707–1957	1957
G. F. Timpson	Et Virtutem: essays on Mill Hill	1957

GEOLOGY

G. M. Davies	Geology of London and S.E. England	1939
R. L. Sherlock	British Regional Geology: London and Thames Valley	1947
S. W. Wooldridge and D. L. Linton	Structure, surface and drainage in S.E. England	1939

HISTORY

Golders Green

F. Howkins	Story of Golders Green and its remarkable development	[1923]

Hampstead Garden Suburb

Dame Henrietta Barnett	A Garden Suburb at Hampstead	1905
Dame Henrietta Barnett	The Story of the growth of the Hampstead Garden Suburb, 1907–1928	1928
Hampstead Garden Suburb Residents Association	Illustrated history of Hampstead Garden	1954
Mrs Arthur Wilson	Wyldes and its story	1904

Hendon

N. G. Brett-James	The Story of Hendon: Manor and Parish	1931
N. G. Brett-James	Some extents and surveys of Hendon	1932–7
Emily S. Capper	Recollections of Hendon in the fifties (Typewritten copy of manuscript)	1925
E. T. Evans	The History and topography of the Parish of Hendon	1890
T. H. G. Giles	The Administration of poor rate relief . . . during the eighteenth century. (Typewritten script)	1959
J. E. Walker	Hendon 1851–1951	1951

Mill Hill, Edgware, Burnt Oak

T. P. Barker	Edgware and Whitchurch	n.d.
C. F. Baylis	Short history of Edgware and Stanmore in the Middle Ages	1957
N. G. Brett-James	The Story of Mill Hill Village	n.d.
A. G. Clarke	The Story of Goldbeaters and Watling	1931
D. G. Denoon	How Mill Hill got its name	1932
D. G. Denoon and T. Roberts	The Extent of Edgware. A.D. 1277	1933
Ruth Durrant	Watling: a survey of social life on a new housing estate	1939
E. S. Harris and P. N. Molloy	The Watling Community Association: the first twenty-one years	1949
T. J. Relf	Ye Booke of Olde Edgware	1924
W. S. Tootell	A brief sketch of the town of Edgware (Typewritten copy of a manuscript)	1817

INDUSTRY

W. Page, editor	Victoria County History of Middlesex, Volume 2	1911
D. H. Smith	Industries of Greater London	1933

LOCAL GOVERNMENT

Hendon Rural Sanitary Authority	Bye-laws	1877

Hendon Local Board	Bye-laws	1881
Hendon Urban District Council	H.U.D.C. Act	1929
	Minutes	1924–32
	Standing Orders	n.d.
	Proposed extension of boundaries	1928–9
	Register of Electors	1901 to date
Hendon Borough Council	Charter Handbook	1932
	Standing Orders (current edition)	
	Bye-laws (in force)	
	Minutes	1932 to date

NATURAL HISTORY

W. E. Glegg	History of the birds of Middlesex	1935
S. T. Klein	Lepidoptera and Hymenoptera of Middlesex	1887
London Natural History Society	Birds of the London area since 1900	1957
The London Naturalist	The Journal of the London Natural History Society	1927 to date
H. Trimen and W. T. T. Dyer	Flora of Middlesex	1869

PLACE NAMES

D. G. Denoon	How Mill Hill got its name	1932
English Place Names Society, Volume XVIII	The Place Names of Middlesex	1942
J. E. B. Gover	The Place Names of Middlesex	1922

A number of articles and correspondence from local newspapers on the subject of local place names is kept in the local history collection. In addition, there are some interesting but rather speculative suggestions included in F. Hitchin Kemp's Notes on the Survey of Hendon of 1754.

The Dissenters' Grammar School, now Mill Hill School.

Tenterden Hall, built on the traditional site of the original Manor House, now demolished.

MAPS

1597	Plan of Edgware Woods (Photostat)
1754	James Crow. Plan of the Manor and Parish of Hendon
1783	Isaac Messeder. Plan of the Manor and Parish of Hendon (Photostat)
1796	John Cooke. Map of the Manor and Parish of Hendon
c.1800	R. H. Jago. Plan of the Manor and Parish of Hendon (Photostat)
1828	F. Whishaw. Map of the whole Manor and Parish of Hendon

The Ordnance Survey maps on both 6 in. and 25 in. to the mile scales, covering the whole area from 1864 to the current edition which is still in progress, are bought as they become available. A number of specialized maps and estate plans, and maps of smaller areas, are also kept in the local history collection.

PERIODICALS

Newspapers and magazines are a valuable source for local history, and a number of these (including church, school, ratepayers and residents' association magazines) are filed in the local history collection. The most important source however, is the file of the *Hendon & Finchley Times*, for which the dates 1891 to 1925 are covered with occasional gaps, and from 1925 to the present date in unbroken sequence.

FURTHER READINGS

For those readers who would like advice and help in the study of local history the following publications are recommended:

F. Evans and others	Local studies for schools	1949
Historical Association	English Local History handlist	1952
W. G. Hoskins	Local History in England	1959

Library Association, County Libraries Section	Readers' guide to books on the sources of local history	1959
W. C. Tate	The Parish Chest	1946?
J. West	Village Records	1962

FLYING AT HENDON

On the evening of 26 August 1862 farm labourers working at Mill Hill were startled to see a balloon bearing five passengers descending from the sky. It had taken off from the Crystal Palace a few hours earlier on a journey to Biggleswade. This, the first record of a flight to and from Hendon, has been taken as an opening point for the exhibition.

Soon after the turn of the century Mr E. I. Everett, a director of the Colindale firm of Everett, Edgecumbe & Co. Ltd, built and flew his own aircraft from a temporary shed on a field between the Midland Railway and Edgware Road. This machine ended its maiden flight in a tree and was afterwards referred to as 'The Grasshopper'.

The real story of flying at Hendon began in April 1910 when Louis Paulhan and Claude Grahame-White entered for the £10,000 *Daily Mail* prize offered by Lord Northcliffe for the first flight made from London to Manchester in one day. Mr Everett placed his field at the disposal of the French aviator who duly carried off the prize, while Grahame-White made his unsuccessful attempt from Wormwood Scrubs.

'Dick' Fairey, who as a young man experimented with model aeroplanes in the old brickfields at Finchley Lane, won the Aero Models Silver Cup at the Crystal Palace in August of the same year. He later became Sir Richard Fairey, M.B.E., head of the great firm that has produced the Fairey Delta 2, one time holder of the world speed record.

In the meantime Grahame-White had discovered in Hendon the acres of flat pasture-land north-west of the Midland Railway, and decided that, at the right time, he would form a centre of aeronautics there. In December 1910 he acquired the field from which Louis Paulhan had started for the London to Manchester flight, and with his friend Richard T. Gates began to clear the ground for what was later to become London Aerodrome, Hendon.

The Grahame-White Aviation Company was formed in 1911 and a flying school established there. The first event was a flying display organized under the auspices of the Parliamentary Aerial Defence Committee to demonstrate the military possibilities of the aeroplane. During the summer of 1911 the First United Kingdom Aerial Post was inaugurated and over 130,000 letters and postcards were flown between Hendon and Windsor.

By 1912 regular weekend flying meetings were held, with closed circuit races round pylons and night flying exhibitions. The first Aerial Derby was flown on 8 June and won by T. O. M. Sopwith in a Bleriot monoplane – his official time for the course of eighty-one miles being one hour twenty-three minutes and eight seconds.

Successful machines were built in the Grahame-White Factory during 1913 and 1914, notably a passenger-carrying biplane which on one occasion flew for nineteen minutes with nine passengers – world record at the time.

At the outbreak of war in 1914 the Grahame-White Flying School at Hendon was impressed by the Admiralty for the purpose of training naval pilots. A flight of aeroplanes was stationed there for the aerial defence of London, pilots of this flight also acting as instructors at the flying school. The first recorded ascent at night for the purpose of defending London was made in September 1914 but the flight was without incident. A Sopwith aircraft took off from Hendon on the night of the first Zeppelin raid on London, 31 May 1915, but crashed at Hatfield and the pilot and observer were both killed. About this time Grahame-White was allowed to relinquish his naval commission so that he might devote his attention to the building of aircraft and the training of pilots at Hendon.

Sporting and passenger flying were resumed after the war when the London Flying Club was established. The Club house is now the Headquarters of the Metropolitan Police College. The King's Cup Air Race began its career at Hendon and the first of the Royal Air Force Pageants was held there in 1921 while the aerodrome was still owned by the Grahame-White Company.

In 1923 the Air Ministry requisitioned the aerodrome and it became a station for training and communication flights. Between the wars the annual Air Pageant helped to foster air sense and spirit in the British public, and airmen recorded in the programmes as taking part in the aerobatic displays were later to become aces of the second World War.

The Society of British Aircraft Constructors used Hendon Aerodrome for their Trade Show between 1932 and 1936. This event was moved to Hatfield in 1937 and is now held at Farnborough.

During the second World War, fighters were stationed at Hendon until 1940 when the station was relegated to training and transport. Many historic flights were made from Hendon, including Mr Churchill's dramatic journey to France in 1940 and Count Bernadotte's armistice mission to the German High Command in 1945. The Station is now used for training purposes by both the Royal Air Force and American Army Air Force.

Hendon Aerodrome was not the only centre of flying in Hendon, for in 1912 Handley Page Limited moved their works and aerodrome from Barking to Cricklewood. From then until 1929 the famous series of Handley Page heavy aircraft, both civil and military, were designed, built and flown at Cricklewood. Growth of building round the aerodrome however forced the company to move its flying ground to Radlett in 1929. The works are still at Cricklewood where such aircraft as the Halifax, Hastings, Hermes and Victor were designed and constructed, but assembly and testing are now done at Radlett.

Just outside the western borders of the Borough, at their works in Stag Lane, the de Havilland Aircraft Company (now part of the Bristol Siddeley Group) have been operating since 1920, although the team which was to create this great company was assembling from 1914 onwards in the works of the Aircraft Manufacturing Company at the Hyde. In 1920 this company went out of business and the de Havilland Aircraft Company was formed, occupying in the first instance two sheds and two huts at Stag Lane. The novelist, Nevil Shute, at one time a designer for the firm, has written an amusing account of these proceedings in his autobiography *Slide Rule*. From these beginnings grew the company that produced the Moth, the Mosquito, the Vampire, the Venom and the Comet.

Amy Johnson learnt to fly at the London Aeroplane Club at Stag Lane and in 1930 flew a Moth to Australia. Sir Alan Cobham, who was associated with the de Havilland Aircraft Company in its early days, used the Stag Lane Aerodrome for the National Aviation display in 1932.

The Company's main works and aerodrome have now moved to Hatfield and Stag Lane Aerodrome, like the Handley Page field at Cricklewood, is built over.

LANDMARKS IN THE DEVELOPMENT
OF HENDON

1851–1963

1851
Pop. (Census) 3333. 500 inhabited houses.
Edgware pop. (Census) 765.
Act to enable the Regents Canal Co. to enlarge the Brent Reservoir.

1852

1853
No street lighting in Hendon – residents carried colza oil lamps after dark.
Enlargement of Brent Reservoir by Regents Canal Co.

1854
Charity Schools existed at Church End, Hendon and Mill Hill. (Founded eighteenth century)

1855
Hendon Fire Brigade formed.
Hendon Congregational Church, Brent Street, built.

1856
Childs Hill National School opened.
Horse buses operating along Edgware Road to Edgware.
All Saints Church, Childs Hill, built.

1857
Merryweather manual fire engine purchased from the Metropolitan Fire Brigade.

1858

1859
Lower Welsh Harp Tavern rebuilt.

1860

1861

1862
Horse races held at Welsh Harp.
Beginning of organized water supply for Hendon.

1863
38 Farms on Hendon ordnance survey map.
Our Lady of Dolours Church, Hendon, rebuilt.
Official scheme for the administration of Hendon Charities.

1864
Toll gate erected on Edgware Road at end of Deansbrook Lane.

1865

1866
Hendon Volunteer Fire Brigade formed.
Hendon included in the limits of water supply of the West Middlesex
Water-Works Company.
Vaccination order at Edgware.
Holcombe House, Mill Hill, became St Joseph's Foreign Missionary
College.

1867
Dame School at Vine Cottage, Cricklewood Lane.
Edgware, Highgate and London Railway cut through Dole Street
Farm.

1868
G.N.R. (L.N.E.R.) built railway line to Edgware through Goldbeaters.
Midland Railway opened.

1869
Mill Hill School reconstituted.

1870
Childs Hill British day school opened.
Jimmy Bushnell's omnibus ran daily from Hendon to the G.P.O.
A horse omnibus plied regularly between Hendon and Oxford Street via Cricklewood.
Mr Woolley's coach and Mr Sutton's teams travelled from Mill Hill to Town.
Voluntary education rate began.

1871
Pop. (Census) 6972.
Gas lighting Childs Hill and Hendon.

1872
Edgware Road ceased to be a turnpike.
Hendon under jurisdiction of Edgware Sanitary Authority.
Parish Constables Act.

1873
Water supply for Hendon from Town Pump in Brent Street, for the Hyde from the pump at the Hyde Brewery, Edgware from a well near the Parish Church.
Water sellers delivered water at 1*d* to 2*d* per pail.
Colne Valley Water Co. obtained Parliamentary power to supply water in that part of Hendon defined in their Act.
Hendon Baptist Church, Finchley Lane, opened.
Enlargement of St Mary's Churchyard.

1874

1875
Hendon & Finchley Times established.

1876
Last parish meeting held at the Greyhound Inn.
Experiment made with a mechanical hare in a field near the Welsh Harp.

1877
Hendon Rural Sanitary Authority issued bye-laws.

1878

1879
Hendon Local Government Board formed.
Hendon constituted an urban Sanitary Authority.
Local Government district divided into 3 wards for the election of 12 members. (6 Hendon, 3 Childs Hill, 3 Mill Hill)
Hendon Debating Society founded.

1880
Hendon Local Government Board Act.
'Fish' Smart (England's Champion skater) at the Welsh Harp.
First Amateur Skating Championship of Hendon held at the Welsh Harp.
Golders Green Gazette established.

1881
Pop. (Census) 10,484.
Christ Church, Brent Street, built.
Hendon Local Board Bye-laws issued.
Mill Hill Cricket Club founded.
First part-time Medical Officer of Health appointed.

1882
Provisional Order for compulsory purchase of lands for sewage disposal.
Casting competition at the Welsh Harp.
Sunnyhill Gardens (now Sunningfields Crescent) built.

1883
Parish Lock up, Bell Lane sold.
Lending Library at Fuller Street and another as part of the activities of the Co-operative movement.

1884
Hendon Railway Bill.
Provisional Order for acquisition of land for sewage disposal.

1885
Cobden-Sanderson, book-binder, came to Goodyers, Brent Street.
'Littleberries', the Ridgeway, Mill Hill, opened as St Vincent's Orphanage.
Hendon (Middlesex) Building Society established.
Hendon came within Finchley Parliamentary District.
Bazalgette Report recommended the construction of a main intercepting sewer.

1886
First main sewage outfall works opened.
Provisional Order for compulsory purchase of lands for street improvements.
Primrose League inaugurated.

1887
Privy Council licensed cattle market at Edgware.
Butcher's Lane renamed Queens Road.
Mr Gladstone inspected main drainage works at Hendon.

1888

1889
Brampton Grove cut.
Sub fire station opened at Mill Hill.
Parish books transferred from Vestry to Hendon Local Board.
Roman antiquities found at the Grove, the Burroughs.
Hendon Hall a school for girls.
Model Farm built at Church End.
William Morris opened the last public debate of the Hendon Debating Society.

1890
Hendon came within the Harrow Parliamentary District.
Infectious Diseases Hospital opened at 'Old Hospital field allotments'.

1891
Pop. (Census) 15,843.

1892

Parliamentary powers to extend underground to Hampstead and Golders Green.

1893

Last entry in Church Wardens' account books.

1894

Hendon Volunteer Fire Brigade took part in a procession through Hampstead and Hendon on Guy Fawkes Day.

1895

Urban District Council formed (3 wards, 15 members).
Sub fire station opened at Childs Hill.
Lending Library at Church House opened.
A four-in-hand on the ice at the Welsh Harp.
Council offices at the Old Workhouse, the Burroughs.

1896

Order of Local Government Board conferring powers of Parish Council as to Charities.
St John's Church, West Hendon, erected.
Greyhound Inn demolished and rebuilt.

1897

Hendon School Board formed and voluntary education rate ceased.
Order of Local Government Board conferring certain powers of Parish Council on Urban District Council.

1898

Central London Sick Asylum opened. (Now Colindale Hospital.)
Linen & Woollen Drapers' Institution opened in Hammers Lane.

1899

Finchley, Hendon & District Light Railway schemes rejected.
U.D.C. took control of fire protection.
Hendon Congregational Brass Band performed in Brent Street enclosure.
Hendon Electric Lighting Order granted to a Company (confirmed

by the Hendon Electric Lighting Order Confirmation [No. 19] Act,
1899), but transferred to the Council by Deed dated 11 September
1899.

1900
First permanent fire officer appointed.
Sub Fire stations opened at Burnt Oak, West Hendon, Golders Green.
Laying of foundation stone of U.D.C. offices (now Town Hall).
Drill Hall, Algernon Road, opened by the Duke of Cambridge.
Hendon Golf Club founded.

1901
Pop. (Census) 22,450.
Town Hall opened (then U.D.C. offices).
First Board School (Burnt Oak) opened in February and Bell Lane.
Algernon Road and Childs Hill later in the year.
Rateable value £154,398.

1902
West Middlesex Waterworks Co. transferred to Metropolitan Water
Board.
Coronation (Edward VII) festivities in Sunny Hill Fields.
Golders Green Crematorium opened.

1903
Work begun on Hampstead – Golders Green tube extension.
Hendon (Queen's) Park opened.
Hendon Electric Lighting Order, 1899 Amendment Order.
Overflow of Welsh Harp caused by incessant rain flooded the valley
of the Brent.

1904
Electric tram service extended to Canons Park.

1905
First new house built in Golders Green.
Charing Cross, Euston, Hampstead Railway Act.
First fire steamer purchased and stationed opposite Parish Church.
Pound still exists at Edgware near Atkinson's Almshouses.

1906

Hampstead Garden Suburb Act.

1907

Golders Green tube station opened.

First fire hydrants installed.

Mill Hill Queen's Nursing Association for the poor founded.

1908

Electric Lighting Amending Order.

80 houses in the Garden Suburb.

Golders Green football club founded.

1909

La Sagesse Convent School opened.

Golders Lodge demolished and 3 roads (Golders Gardens, Gainsborough Gardens, Powis Gardens) erected on the site.

1910

King George V and Queen Mary visited the Garden Suburb.

Hampstead Garden Suburb Free Church erected.

Grahame-White flying school established at Hendon aerodrome.

Golders Green Chamber of Commerce formed.

1911

Pop. (Census) 38,806.

Coronation Aerial Post took off from Hendon aerodrome.

Church of Saint Jude on the Hill (Garden Suburb) dedicated.

Parliamentary Demonstration held at Hendon Aerodrome.

1912

Fire alarms first installed in the district.

Motor buses operating on two daily routes – 83 from Golders Green to Station Road – 13 from 'The Bell' to London Bridge.

Handley Page Ltd, the first company to be constituted exclusively for the design and manufacture of aeroplanes, moved to Cricklewood.

Ravensfield Manor, the Burroughs, demolished – London Transport bus garage erected on the site.

Prince Albert Inn, Golders Green, rebuilt.

1913

Hendon Court House opened.

Last entry in Vestry minute books.

Hendon Cottage Hospital opened.

Provisional Order for acquisition of land for sewage disposal.

Anna Pavlova at Ivy House, Golders Green.

Fete of Flowers and Aviation at Hendon Aerodrome.

1914

Combined swimming bath and public library contemplated at the Burroughs.

Hendon Fire Station opened at the Burroughs.

Golders Green Hippodrome opened.

St Michael's Church, Golders Green, erected.

1915

Military hospital established at the Club House, Willifield Green Garden Suburb.

Sir Stamford Raffles tomb found in Hendon Churchyard during excavations for the enlargement of the Church.

Urban district divided into 6 Wards.

1916

Alexandra Club, West Hendon entertained wounded soldiers.

Last Court of the Manor of Hendon held at the Whitebear Inn.

1917

The King (George V) and Queen visited the Grahame-White Company factory at Hendon.

Aerodrome at Cricklewood taken over by Handley Page.

Manor House Hospital opened.

1918

First ambulance subscribed by the Hendon Special Constabulary,

King George V and Queen Mary visited 'St Jude on the Hill' Church Garden Suburb.

First flights made from Cricklewood Aerodrome as follows:

(A) over London with 42 passengers, (B) to India in a twin-engined machine, (C) to India in a four-engined machine.

1919
Libraries Acts adopted.
First Libraries Committee appointed.
Victory Aerial Derby held at Hendon Aerodrome.
First London–Paris air passenger service from Cricklewood Aerodrome
Hendon Parliamentary Division formed.

1920
Aerial Derby held at Hendon Aerodrome.
Shire Hall, Shirehall Lane, demolished.
First air meeting after World War I held at Cricklewood.
First full-time Medical Officer of Health appointed.

1921
Pop. (Census) 57,529.
Hendon Women's Club formed.
First Royal Air Force aerial pageant.
Hendon (Middlesex) Building Society terminated.
Bed of Silk Stream diverted.

1922
Hendon War Memorial unveiled.
Sub fire station closed at West Hendon.
St Michael and All Angels Church dedicated (Mill Hill).
Mill Hill Operatic & Dramatic Society formed.
First Swimming Bath opened at West Hendon.
Golders Green Synagogue consecrated.
Abolition of copyhold tenure – Manor Courts ceased to function.
Extensions to isolation hospital.

1923
King's Cup circuit of Britain: aeroplane race took off from Hendon
Aerodrome.
Hendon Central tube station opened.

1924
Mill Hill Park opened.
Edgware tube station opened.
L.C.C. obtained possession of Goldbeaters Farm estate for town

St Mary's, the ancient parish church of Hendon.

St Margarets, the ancient parish church of Edgware.

planning project (now Watling Estate).
Watford by-pass construction began at Finchley Road.
Barnet by-pass under construction.
Juvenile Employment Bureau formed.
Police traps for motorists along Golders Green Road resulted in
hundreds of convictions.

1925

All Souls Unitarian Church, Golders Green, opened.
Carnegie grant of £7,000 promised for library building.
Hendon section of North Circular Road, built.
Jubilee of *Hendon & Finchley Times*.
Dust destructor provided.
Extensions to Hendon Cottage Hospital.

1926

Constructional work began on Watling Estate.
Imposition of first library rate.
Finchley Bridge, Finchley Lane, constructed.
Hendon, Cricklewood & Golders Green Gazette issued Daily News
Sheets during the General Strike.
Counties of Hertford and Middlesex Order.
Hendon Traders' Association formed (now Hendon Chamber of
Commerce).
Great North Way built.
Finchley Road to North Circular Road section of Watford by-pass
opened.
Edgware Literary Society founded.
British Shopping Week held.

1927

First cottage let on Watling Estate.
School libraries service inaugurated.
Fire sub-station at Golders Green closed.
Bunn's Bridge, Mill Hill, constructed over road and railway.
Our Lady of Dolours' church, Hendon, rebuilt.
St Alphage Church, Burnt Oak, erected.
Golders Green Synagogue consecrated.

Orange Hill House demolished.

North Circular Road to N.W. boundary of Hendon section of Watford by-pass opened.

Rotary Club of Hendon founded.

Redhill County Hospital built.

1928

Metropolitan Water Board authorized the laying of large mains to cope with demand for water from Garden Suburb.

Stoneyfields Bridge, Mill Hill, constructed.

Garden Suburb Coming-of-Age celebrations.

School opened on Watling Estate.

Watling Residents Association formed.

1929

Hendon Urban District Council Act.

Central Library opened.

Mill Hill Fire Station opened.

Moat Mount Golf Course purchased by the Council.

Church of Annunciation, Burnt Oak, opened by Cardinal Bourne.

South Lodge, Golders Green, demolished.

Handley Page aerodrome at Cricklewood closed.

Mill Hill Historical Society formed.

Elementary School teaching staff 249, 35 school departments average attendance 7,159.

Isolation hospital opened at Goldsmith Avenue.

1930

4,018 dwellings on Watling Estate.

West Hendon Baptist Church opened.

St Mary's Parish Church – Norman Chancel discovered during reconstruction.

Tenterden Hall, formerly Hendon Place, a school for boys.

Concealed cupboard discovered in Parish Clerk's cottage – contained two very old offertory plates.

Slipper baths opened at Childs Hill and West Hendon.

Rotary Club of Edgware formed.

Dollis Farm demolished.

1931

Pop. (Census) 115,682.

Edgware Parish becomes part of Hendon.

Central Library approved by Master of the Rolls as Repository for Manorial documents.

Urban district 9 wards, Council 33 members.

Church of the Annunciation School, Burnt Oak, opened.

Metropolitan Water Board supplies water to 3,863 acres in the urban district.

Mutton Bridge, Bell Lane, demolished for road widening and rebuilt.

Hendon Juvenile Organizations historical pageant in Hendon Park.

Cowhouse Farm demolished.

Highfield, Golders Green, demolished.

Uphill Farm, Lawrence Street, demolished.

Plough Inn, Holcombe Hill, demolished.

Station Road, Edgware, reconstructed.

Hydro-gliding on the Welsh Harp.

Edgware and Little Stanmore Nursing Association formed.

Edgware Chamber of Commerce formed.

New wing of Manor House Hospital opened by Duke of York.

Total length of public highways about 112 miles.

1932

Hendon became a Borough by Charter of Incorporation.

9 wards, 9 aldermen, 27 councillors (3 for each ward).

Area 10,471 acres, length about 7·3 miles, breadth about 3·6 miles.

Over 1,000 dwellings in Council housing estates.

Hendon County School extended.

La Sagesse Convent's new school building opened by Cardinal Bourne.

Claremont Free (Baptist) Church opened.

British Museum Newspaper Repository opened.

White Bear Inn demolished and rebuilt.

Ambassador Cinema (now the Gaumont), Hendon Central, opened.

Ritz Cinema, Edgware, opened.

First Civil Air Display (Society of British Aircraft Constructors) held at Hendon Aerodrome.

National Aviation Day Display at Hendon aerodrome.

Rateable value £1,424,720.

1933
New Pay Block extension opened at Hendon Cottage Hospital.
Official opening of Watling Community Centre by the Prince of Wales.
Prince George (later Duke of Kent) visits the Express Dairy's depot at Cricklewood.
Church of St Alban and Martyr erected at Golders Green.
Improvements to banks of River Brent in Hendon.
Mill Hill Farm demolished.
Colindeep Lane reconstructed.
Concert in aid of the Mayor's Fund for the Unemployed held at the Ambassador Cinema.
Capitol Cinema, Mill Hill, opened.
Hendon retains the Garden Suburb.

1934
First Honorary Freeman of the Borough (Lt. Col. F. W. Hearn, O.B.E.).
Town Hall extended.
Metropolitan Police College – laying of foundation stone.
The Burroughs Almshouses (the old workhouse, Council Offices) demolished.
Grove House, The Burroughs, demolished.
Last entry in the Court Books for the Manor of Hendon, 8 August.
Welsh Harp Sports Stadium opened.

1935
Golders Green Library opened.
Empire Air Day held at Hendon Aerodrome.
Brent Modern School opened by Princess Louise.
Metropolitan Police College opened.
Brook Lodge, Golders Green Road, demolished.
Decoy Farm demolished.
Vine Cottages (formerly Orange Tree Public House) demolished.
Parish Clerk's wooden cottage demolished and rebuilt in brick.
Hendon Way Hotel built.
Mill Hill swimming bath opened.

1936
Copthall County School opened.

John Keble Church erected at Mill Hill
Hendon Planning Scheme No. 1 came into operation.

1937
Pop. (Est.) 162,079.
Mill Hill library opened.
Mill Hill Health Centre opened.
Excavations for Roman antiquities at Sulloniacae (Brockley Hill).
Hendon Methodist Church rebuilt.
Dole Street Farm demolished.
Three Crowns Inn, Highwood Hill, demolished.
Elementary School teaching staff 415, 45 school departments, average attendance 13,048.
Two Organizers of Physical Training appointed.

1938
Montrose Playing Fields, Burnt Oak, opened.
Edgware Junior and Infant School opened.
Subway under Watford Way, Mill Hill, opened.
Grove Park opened.
Burton Bank, The Ridgeway, Mill Hill, demolished.
King Alfred Junior School, Golders Green, opened.
Empire Air Day at Hendon Aerodrome.
Extensions to Redhill County Hospital.
Henrietta Barnett Junior School opened by H.R.H. Queen Mary.
Last Parish Constable appointed.

1939
Pop. (Est.) 169,765.
1,290 dwellings on Council housing estates.
Dollis Junior and Infant School opened.
Royal Observer Corps Post established at Elstree.
Hendon Technical College building completed but used for Civil Defence purposes during the war.
Hendon Synagogue consecrated.
Gloucester Lodge demolished.
Hendon Women's Club closed.

Odeon Cinema, the Quadrant, opened.
Hendon Planning Scheme No. 2 came into operation.
Bomber crashed in Heading Street on day of outbreak of war.

1940
Mill Hill Library bombed.
All Saints Church, Childs Hill, burnt out.
Emergency Information Service in operation with H.Q. at the Central Library.
'Rout the Rumour' rally held in Hendon Park.
Hendon Welfare and Comforts Organization H.Q .at Central Library.
Hendon Four Fighter fund opened at the Central Library.
Government Lymph Establishment at Colindale.

1941
Her Majesty the Queen visited the Town Hall and Central Library.
Hendon Meals Service operated from the Central Library.
First Special evacuation scheme prepared.
First British Restaurant (St Johns) opened at West Hendon.
Hendon Air Raid Distress Fund inaugurated by the Mayor.

1942
Warship Week and War Weapons Week sponsored by the Mayor of Hendon.
British Restaurants opened at the Hyde and Golders Green (St Michaels)
Hendon Food Production Week at Burroughs Playing Fields.

1943
Pop. (Est.) 132,837
'Victoria' British Restaurant opened in Brent Street, 'Montrose' at Burnt Oak, 'Granville' at Childs Hill and 'Edgeworth' Edgware.
Hendon Show held in the Burroughs Playing Fields.

1944
Pop. (Ration Books) 135,344.
Boundary Commission for England report on . . . abnormally large constituencies.
Invasion defence scheme prepared.

'Fortune' British Restaurant opened at Temple Fortune and 'Hartley' at Mill Hill.
Holiday attractions in Hendon and Watling Parks.
Church Farm purchased by the Council.

1945
Pop. (Ration Books) 140,000.
Public meeting on Post War Development.
1,100 properties held under requisition.
Hendon Operatic & Choral Society formed.
Entertainments in the parks.
Hendon Parliamentary Borough divided into North and South divisions.

1946
Pop. (Ration Books) 151,000.
Collision on London Transport's Northern Line at Edgware.
Hendon & District Music Society formed.
Entertainments in the parks.

1947
Travelling Library Service inaugurated.
Excavations for Roman antiquities at Sulloniacae (Brockley Hill).
Entertainments in the parks.

1948
Pop. (Ration Books) 160,000.
Road Safety Week.
Borough Horticultural Show held in the Burroughs Playing Fields.

1949
Pop. (Ration Books) 157,000.
Travelling Library Service extended.
Gramophone Record Library opened.
Mill Hill Preservation Society formed.
Last civic restaurants closed.

1950

Pop. (Ration Books) 156,000.
Temporary Library opened in Truth Hall, Edgware.
Site for permanent library at Edgware acquired.
Medical Research Council Library opened at Mill Hill.
Bittacy House, Mill Hill, demolished.
Hendon Arts Council formed.
Hendon Show held in Mill Hill Park.

1951

Pop. Ration Books 155,690 (30.4.51), Census 155,835 (8.4.51).
42,000 houses and flats.
4,110 homes on Watling Estate.
Common Room at Layfield Close Dwellings for Aged Persons opened.
County of Middlesex development plan.
Inglis Barracks, Mill Hill, re-opened as a basic training unit for recruits of the Middlesex Regiment.
Civil Aircraft accident (Dakota G–AGIW) at Mill Hill.
Civic open air theatre in Hendon Park between 5 June and 15 September.
Festival of Britain Celebrations.
Hendon Show held in Hendon Park.
Rateable value £2,004,207
Territorial and Auxiliary Forces Units adoption by Hendon Council.

1952

Edgware Library opened.
1,298 dwellings erected by Council since 1954.
All Saints Church, Childs Hill, rebuilt.
Sodium Lighting installed at junction of Hodford Road and the Vale.
42,024 houses and flats in Hendon.
Hendon Show held in Hendon Park.
1939–45 addition to Hendon War Memorial unveiled.

1953

Travelling Library Service extended.
Watling Association Silver Jubilee.

1954
Lord Mayor of London, Sir Noel Bowater, opened 14 new alms-houses at junction of Kingsbury Road and Buck Lane, called Bowater Close.

Completion of first Queensbury Parish Church at cost of £44,000.

All Saints Church at Waltham Drive, consecrated by Bishop of Willesden.

New Wing (Coronation Wing) opened at Colindale Hospital.

Burnt Oak Library opened.

Visit of Duchess of Gloucester to present prizes to student nurses at Royal National Orthopaedic Hospital at Stanmore.

Alderman Clemens picked as Sheriff of Middlesex by Queen Mother.

3 new freemen of the Borough, Lord Latham, Alderman Naar, Leonard Worden (Town Clerk).

£50,000 extension of Kingsbury Maternity Hospital opened by Princess Margaret.

Princess Margaret also visited Boreham Wood to lay foundation stone of St Michael and All Angels Church on Theobald Estate.

Queen's visit to Boy Scout Gang Show at Hippodrome.

Queen Mother opened Highwood House as a Red Cross home for the aged.

Duke of Edinburgh visited National Institute for Medical Research.

1955
Church Farm House Museum opened by Major N. G. Brett-James.

New physiotherapy unit opened at Manor House Hospital – gift of Busmen's Friendly Society.

Old folks home opened on site of All Saints Vicarage, Childs Hill.

Spur Road skyscraper flats scheme adopted by Council.

Window dedicated to Harold Holt Lea unveiled at Edgware Parish Church.

1956
Dedication of St Michael's Church, Childs Hill.

Visit of Queen Mother to Stanmore Orthopaedic Hospital.

New £22,000 X-ray dept. opened at Manor House Hospital.

£54,000 scheme to widen Sanders Lane Bridge, Mill Hill.

1957
Opening of new dept. at Manor House Hospital.
Visit of Prince Philip to Handley Page.
Visit of Princess Margaret to Garden Suburb.
Queen visited Mill Hill School on prize day.
Planning of smokeless zone in Edgware, to extend from Canons Park to Elstree boundary.
Travelling library services extended to Kenilworth Estate and Temple Fortune.

1958
New polio research centre opened at Hendon Isolation Hospital.
Queen Mother visited flats at Spur Road.
Plans for subway and reconstruction of roundabout at Mill Hill Circus and at junction with Hartley Avenue and Watford Way.

1959
Proposed plan for Mill Hill synagogue.
Plans for skyscraper flats in New Brent Street, Foster Street, Foster Place and North Street.

1961
Hendon Forming link with Berlin.
Restoration of Christ Church.
Edgware library – new building opened to the public.
Photocharging introduced at Golders Green library.
Completion of St Barnabas Church, Temple Fortune.
New offices erected, High Street, Edgware.
Block of luxury flats to be built on Hendon Hall Hotel Lane.
Holders Hill – 3 Blocks of flats on site of Rydal Mount, Freelands, and Holdersgrath.

1962
Childs Hill branch library opened.
Photocharging introduced at Central Library.
New block opened at Manor House Hospital.
Three-tier flyover at Brent Cross approved by Min. of Transport.

INDEX

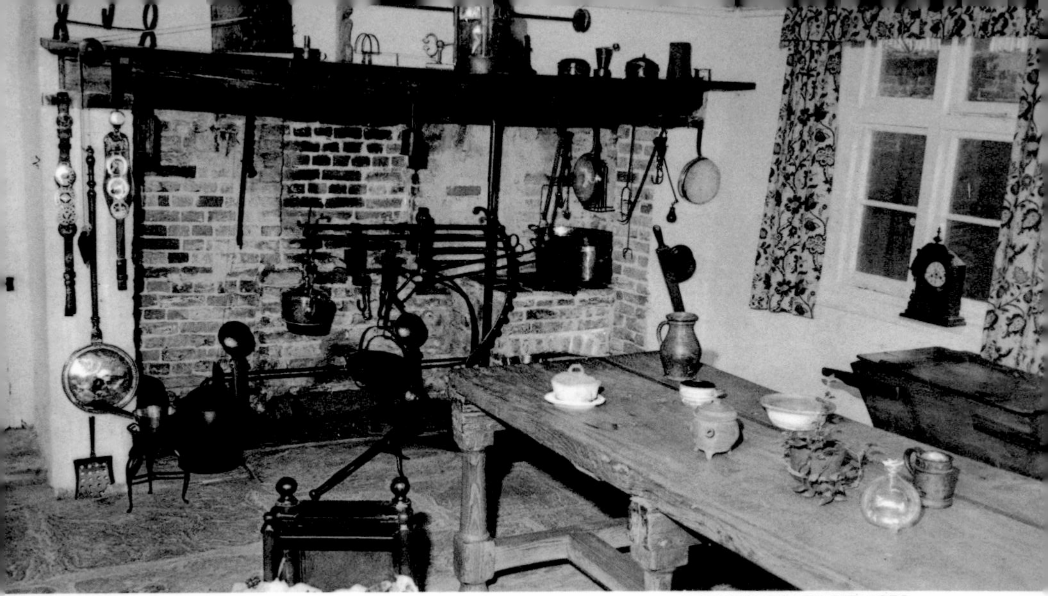

CHURCH FARM HOUSE MUSEUM KITCHEN

BARNET LIBRARY SERVICES

POST CARD

CORRESPONDENCE

ADDRESS